FROM STA

YOUR OWN CONSULTING BUSINESS

By Reg Pirie

Ink Ink Publishing

From Starting to Marketing...
YOUR OWN CONSULTING BUSINESS

Copyright © 1997 by Reg Pirie

All rights reserved. No portion of this publication may be reproduced without written permission from the publisher. These restrictions extend to any means of electronic or mechanical duplication, including: photocopying, recording or other information retention systems.

Published in 1997 by:
Ink Ink Publishing
120 Promenade Circle - Suite 1107
Thornhill, Ontario   Canada L4J 7W9
Tel: 416-230-3241   Fax: 905-771-6668

The author has made every effort to make this book as complete and accurate as possible. It is intended purely as a reference and educational guide for those who are or may be involved in establishing a consulting business.

Neither the publisher nor the author is expressing legal, financial or other professional opinions and readers should seek expert assistance as dictated by their personal and business circumstances.

Canadian Cataloguing in Publication Data

Pirie, Reg, 1948-
        From starting to marketing-- your own consulting business
ISBN 0-9698196-1-7
1. New Business enterprises - Management. 2. Consultants - Marketing. 3. Small business - Management. 4. Entrepreneurship.
I. Title. II. Your own consulting business.

HD62.5.P57 1997   658.1'1   C97-931263-9

TABLE OF CONTENTS

TABLE OF CONTENTS - Continued

PREFACE

So, you have decided to become a consultant.

Some of your associates still working in the corporate jungle may raise a clandestine eyebrow after you proclaim your new career direction. Others will envy your decision but will also be the first to admit the perilous life of an independent consultant is not for them. The reactions from friends, family, business peers and a host of others will vary greatly. However, the reality of the situation is that you are embarking on an adventure that is not recommended for the faint of heart. On the other hand, you have an opportunity to control your own destiny and to achieve a sense of satisfaction few ever attain as employees.

Having stepped over the threshold from corporate life to independent consultant, I can appreciate the euphoria and the fear associated with making what is perhaps the biggest decision in your working life. It will not only test your mettle but will dramatically influence all those who are close to you. For better or worse, your life will never be the same. By the way, the "for better or worse" reference was intentional. You are entering into a marriage with a business venture, which will not necessarily be as forgiving as many life partners and will likely be much more demanding.

Let me stop here and attempt to explain why I decided to write this book. If the next few paragraphs strike a harmonizing chord with you, I am certain the following pages will be of great assistance. Conversely, if you see little merit in the next few paragraphs, I would suggest you keep perusing the bookshelves for something more appropriate.

In 1994 I wrote my first book, From Fired.... .....To Hired. It was intended to help the job seeker of the 1990s by taking him or her through a series of logical steps to landing the right new position. But many of my clients, students and those attending presentations were not looking for traditional jobs. They wanted to make the leap to go it on their own. They knew they needed some practical, no-nonsense information about how to get started and how to succeed as a consultant. This book is directed toward those who want to know how to become a successful consultant. It is not written for those who are wrestling with the question, should I or shouldn't I start my own consulting business.

Many of these people had the knowledge, skills, abilities, drive and desire to translate or transfer their experience into a full-time consulting practice. Some even had their first assignment in hand, often from a previous employer in the midst of downsizing, reorganizing, right-sizing or re-engineering. Even those with their first contract looked skeptically to the future, and a small nagging voice always raised the issue of where and how to find work on a continuing basis.

The simple answer is twofold: marketing and networking. Regrettably, few of us are born marketers or networkers. We may possess the technical capabilities to be a consultant, but those credentials do not make us able to acquire new business and maintain existing clients. The business world is scattered with the corpses of failed or failing independent consultants who had the talent to deliver a product or service but lacked the ability and methodology to generate new business while sustaining existing customer relationships.

In the upcoming seventeen chapters I will impart some common-sense information any consultant can use in establishing and maintaining his or her own business. Many of the concepts are taken from practical experience in jointly running and eventually selling a prosperous business. I will share my mistakes (there were a few) and my successes (I would like to think they outnumbered the miscues). I will also offer suggestions that have worked well for many of my entrepreneurial friends.

A word of warning. You may find some of my suggestions picayune. You may want to take some shortcuts. You may want to indulge yourself in only the easy parts of the process. As the well-worn cliché goes — trust me! Paying close attention to detail and being extremely organized are important prerequisites for success. Shortcuts are always enticing, but they seldom get us to where we want to go as quickly as we hoped. And whoever said being a consultant was easy? Come to think of it, the previous sentence is one you will frequently repeat to yourself.

CHAPTER 1

Focus, Organization, Research and Activity
Introduction

If you have read From Fired........ ....To Hired, you may recall my constant reference to four words: Focus, Organization, Research and Activity.

Those words were used to illustrate the four key elements of any successful job search. They are equally applicable to achieving your goals as a consultant. Why? Because the best way to view yourself as a professional consultant is as someone who is constantly seeking a job. The paying contracts you secure are interruptions in your unemployed status.

I have often used this analogy when making presentations to those considering a career change to some form of consulting. Invariably, someone in the audience will challenge me by suggesting my comparison is overly negative.

True, but nothing keeps my business development adrenaline pumping more than the realization I must always be on the prowl for my next assignment. Call it a form of self-motivation. Remember, when you are self-employed, the only person who will spur you on is you. There is no boss sitting in the corner office who is going to summon you for a chat about your lacklustre performance during the last quarter.

With those words of wisdom still resonating, let me set the stage for the methodical approach I recommend for those preparing to launch into self-employment as a consultant. The most logical place to start is by outlining the broad assumptions upon which I have written the book:

1. This book will be most helpful to those who have never been in business for themselves.

2. You, and perhaps a partner, are starting from scratch.

3. You have the requisite skills and needed credentials to be a consultant in your selected field of endeavour.

4. This is a long-term venture and not just something intended to tide you over until a real job comes along.

Item number four is extremely important, because the balance of this book frequently alludes to doing things properly over the long haul. Effectively starting and marketing your business is not something that can be done if in the back of your mind you are viewing the exercise as a temporary solution to unemployment. Commitment, better still dogged commitment is a trait that will set you apart from the pretenders.

So how do you tackle this seemingly monumental task? Indeed, how do I help you develop a game plan that will enhance your chances to meet and exceed your personal career and business expectations? First, you will want to spend a few moments reflecting on the words focus, organization, research and activity. From here on in, everything you do should be associated with one or all of those words.

Then you may wish to consider other choice words and phrases that begin to describe your vision of a successful consultant. Here are but a few that leap to mind: systematic, logical, persistent, planned, analytical, thoughtful, professional, creative, flexible, dependable, personalized, service-oriented, leading edge, unique, on time, strategic and motivated.

The list is here to cause you to start thinking like a consultant. As you move beyond this chapter you will find out just how important it is to be able to accurately describe yourself, and by extension, your business. It is also interesting to note most newcomers to the consulting game are modest to a fault.

But let's not get too far ahead. To set the stage for the balance of the book, here is a recap of what we are about to cover, and the rationale behind how the information has been organized.

FOCUS

As with any new undertaking, it is critical to have a firm understanding of where you are headed and what you wish to accomplish. It is equally important to have a sense of how you are going to get there and how much work is involved. Ultimately you will want to measure your success.

Achieving your focus is really a two-part process. As an independent consultant, you need to visualize your personal goals, and you must also be able to develop a business plan that will allow you to accomplish those aspirations via your business.

This concept can be a little foreign to those who have been accustomed to employee status. In the past, you could more easily rationalize not achieving personal goals because something beyond your control had happened at work. Company profits were low, therefore you didn't get a raise or a bonus. Your employer restructured, therefore you missed out on a promotion.

Now you have an opportunity to change that. As an independent businessperson, you are not only the employee, you are also the employer. The success of your company will have a direct and immediate impact on you personally and those around you. The old adage, the buck stops here, is poignant and profound when you are in business for yourself.

In an effort to bring some semblance of order to the dilemma created by being both employee and employer, we will assess the two issues separately. The next chapter will attempt to crystalize what you want to achieve from a personal standpoint. It will also allow you to take a hard look at what positive attributes you bring to the table. You will want to honestly determine where you need to enhance and improve yourself to make your new venture enjoyable and profitable.

Once you have a firm handle on what you and your family desire from a personal perspective, we will progress to chapter three which deals with establishing a clear view or focus of what you want your company to look like. By the end of chapter three, you should have a better sense of where you are headed and why.

ORGANIZATION AND RESEARCH

These two components often overlap, so for the time being, let me address them jointly. Once you have established a general direction for yourself and your company, the next step is to get organized. To become organized, you will need to do some research. Depending on your chosen field of specialization, there could well be a great deal of research required.

Based on personal, practical and professional experience, this is where most of us begin to make mistakes. Why? The answer usually can be summed up in two words: excitement and urgency. We become caught up in the thrill of an intriguing new adventure and we have a keen desire to move forward at lightning speed. Often we think, "Such and such is not a pressing issue right now, so I'll skip that step and come back to it later." This approach can create havoc for you.

Let me give you a brief example. The development of a well-thought-out corporate brochure is often an item new entrepreneurs leave for completion at a later date. Trust me: you don't want to be putting together your brochure at midnight because someone has unexpectedly asked you for a copy. A corporate brochure is but one of many documents that should be fully prepared before the open sign is hung outside your office.

Many how-to publications are fast off the mark to offer readers long lists of things to do. The idea has merit. However, for you to make informed decisions, both short-term and long-range, I believe you need some insight about why the questions are being posed. If you know why you must be supremely organized and why meticulous research is so critical, you will be able to move forward with a greater degree of confidence.

ACTIVITY

It's easy to illustrate the need to be sharply focused, carefully organized and well researched. This is due in large measure to the fact that most of our employers urged and taught us to utilize these basic principles of planning and problem solving.

But activity is more abstract, particularly when you might not have a good gauge of how much activity is acceptable or needed. In previous jobs, experience gave you built-in benchmarks, which would allow you to know when you were working at a normal pace and when you were going flat out.

Because you are new to self-employment it is difficult to establish activity guidelines. Now let's be honest. There is a reasonably good chance that one of the appeals to self-employment was the fact you could set your own pace and hours of work. That said, it can be most annoying and distracting if you don't know if you are working hard enough. As such, I have made a genuine effort throughout the book to offer input on how to keep yourself moving forward, bearing in mind the need for a high degree of focused activity.

CHAPTER 2

Focus — What Do I Want?

One of the assumptions of this book is that you have already decided to forge ahead with your own consulting business.

With that fact in mind, this chapter is not going to dwell on the decision-making process. On the other hand, it is important to personally take stock before you get too far along. You and your family need to consider several issues and questions.

Why are you going into business for yourself?

When I pose this question to people I get a variety of answers, for example:

- to get away from big company politics
- to make more money
- to spend more time with the family
- to work fewer hours
- to reduce commuting time
- to avoid being constantly out of town
- to have fun again, doing something I enjoy
- to do things the way I want
- to better prepare for an earlier retirement
- to try something other than working for someone else

These are good answers, and there are truly no rights or wrongs. Indeed, I would encourage you to take a moment and decide if some of these answers reflect your reasons for going into business on your own. You should add to the list if other factors influenced your decision.

Reviewing why you decided to get into business is not simply an exercise to delineate what you wish to achieve. You will want to have this list tucked away so a year from now you can sit back and assess or measure how you are progressing. Don't forget, you are the employer and the employee. As is the case in corporate life there is a need to periodically stop and complete a performance review. From here on in, you are not only the subject of the appraisal but you are also the appraiser.

I don't want to come across as being too cynical, but I did commit that I would offer the benefit of my experiences. The following comments are generalizations but they deserve thought. If you have a significant other and children, I would recommend some open discussion concerning how life is going to change as a result of your decision to enter the world of consulting.

Politics

You will never completely avoid company politics, even if you are an outside consultant. At best, you can walk away from a corporation's political wrangling when you finish a contract. At worst, you must learn how to quickly identify the politically sensitive hot spots. By doing so, you will be able to manoeuvre through those troubled waters to get your job done.

More Money

When it comes to money, the first lesson you will learn is that it is not how much you make but how much you get to keep. I have no reliable statistics to confirm that consultants make more money than peers who are still shackled to an employer. But a self-employed person has greater control over potential earning power. Self-employment does offer the option to enhance your personal revenue generation. You will notice I did not use the word guarantee.

Time

Changing how you spend your time is a very personal issue and one that requires an extraordinary commitment if you want to alter how you have done things in the past. I know a host of consultants, and for the most part I don't believe they have tangibly reduced their hours of work by being self-employed.

Granted, some have reduced commuting time by locating their office closer to home. Others, who were constantly on a plane, have made a conscious decision to seek assignments that do not require major travel commitments. Frankly, many of my consulting associates say they are working harder and longer. But that statement is usually followed by a caveat, indicating they are having more fun and enjoying work again. Why? Because they have greater control and they don't begrudge longer hours if those are self-imposed.

If there is a downside to self-employment, it's finding the time for vacations. In the first couple of years after starting a business, it is exceedingly difficult to carve out time for a holiday. This is most noticeable when you are a one person office. Even if you have the funds to take off, you naturally worry about the phone call from a potential client, who needs you ASAP.

We all need a break now and then. Here are a few suggestions that might allow you to get away to recharge the batteries:

- Most industries have lulls and you might want to plan a week off to coincide with your customers' slow time.

- Always let your existing customers know when you will be gone and for how long.

- If other avenues are not open, you can call forward the phone to the cottage.

What are my personal goals and how will they affect my family?

If you have a significant other, now is the time to have some very honest discussions about what you both want, including personal career aspirations and family objectives. Review the questions noted below. This is not the time to be vague about where you are headed.

- What type of life-style do we want to have?
- Is the life-style we have had different from what we want?
- What after-tax income is required to maintain our life-style?
- What can we get by on while we are building the business?
- What long-term obligations are looming on the horizon (for example, a new car or children's university tuition)?
- How do we factor in continued savings for retirement?
- What major business expenditures are we facing?
- Do we plan to stay in the same home or might this change?
- Will we need to temporarily change our spending habits? Are we ready to make the necessary commitments?
- If some short-term belt-tightening is necessary, how do we explain the changes to the children?
- Do we have enough insurance? Might we need more or different types of coverage?
- When do we want to retire?
- How much personal wealth do we want / need to accumulate?
- After the new business is up and running, what would we like to draw as a salary?
- Do we have the right person to assist us with our personal financial planning?

At this point some authors insert a fancy personal financial planning form for you to fill out. I am going to resist the temptation, because if you are about to open your own consulting practice, you had best know how to fill out a personal monthly budget. You need an extremely good handle on your personal financial situation, because those dollars and cents will influence your business planning process.

There is another reason I avoid including pro forma financial statements. In my opinion, self-employed people must learn how to rely on the experts they select to be part of their professional team. In subsequent chapters we will discuss the need to work closely with an accountant and a financial planner.

I would be remiss if I didn't pen a few observations about the impact starting your own business can have on the junior members of a family. Kids today are smarter than we were, and they usually react to change based on how it will complicate their own lives. So in the mad scramble to get your business off the ground, don't forget to keep the whole family plugged in to what is happening. Hopefully the following questions raised by kids will stick in your mind.

- Five-year-old Annie's question — "Daddy, is Mom really sick? She hasn't left her office in the basement for weeks and she never catches the bus to go to work anymore."

- Eight-year-old Jason's comment — "Why can't we play basketball in the driveway anymore? Dad's just sitting up in his office above the garage playing at his computer."

- Fifteen-year-old Susan's question — "Why can't we go away skiing like we do every year? Absolutely all my friends are going. This would never have happened if you guys hadn't quit your real jobs!"

- Sixteen-year-old David's observation — "Why can't I have a car? All the other parents can afford to buy one for their kids."

- Six-year-old Samantha's contribution — "Don't worry Mom, I'll take care of Daddy when you work late at your new office."

Sometimes your kids can be brutal. When all is said and done, they want to help out just like Samantha — if they understand what is going on. Some families I know have gone as far as enlisting the aid of the kids. Involvement can range from licking envelopes at the home office to having a teenager input data on weekends.

What do I bring to the game?

One of the most difficult tasks we all face is honest self-assessment. At some point in my long career as a Human Resource practitioner, I recall experimenting with a performance review system based exclusively on self-appraisal. I may not have been a totally unbiased observer, but the output was not in keeping with the more quantifiable results collected previously. Some participants were extraordinarily hard on themselves, while others were quick to sing their own praises.

I was always rather ambivalent about performance reviews until I got out on my own. Then it struck me that to be a success, I was going to need to know where I excelled and where I needed to make improvements. Recognizing your positives is a relatively easy task, but zeroing in on and confessing to your less positives can be a sobering experience. Your consulting business will depend on how well you know yourself and how dedicated you are to enhancing yourself.

This chapter is not intended to cause you to query your basic technical abilities and the proficiencies associated with your chosen business. You do, however, want to have a good handle on personal traits, characteristics, skills and abilities deemed essential in your line of work.

Without thinking about yourself, take a few minutes to consider what you envision as minimal requirements for a consultant in your field. You might want to leaf back to chapter one, where we noted a few descriptive words. Using some of those words and others that come to mind, compose your own list of words that describe the ten most critical ingredients associated with your type of consulting practice.

Forgetting about technical qualifications, rank those ten words and phrases from most important to the least. Remember, they are all critical, but some will rank higher than others. Let me lead by example and provide a list that would apply to someone who was entering into the re-employment counselling business.

- accessible *
- flexible
- sympathetic
- honest / forthright
- reliable / dependable
- communicative
- consistent
- attuned to corporate culture *
- service-oriented
- systematic / well organized / on time*

I cheated. A few years after I established myself in the career transition field, I started to ask my corporate clients what was important to them. My list is a distillation of the top ten items uppermost in their minds. During casual conversations with a few of my competitors, I found they thought the list was a good recap of the most noteworthy requirements.

If someone had asked me to compose a list in 1990, I suspect I would not have recorded those words and phrases marked with an asterisk. So there can be differences between what a new consultant believes a client will want and what the client will actually demand of the consultant.

To take the process a step further, look at your list of words and phrases. Here comes the hard part. Rate yourself on a scale of one to ten, ten being the highest, in terms of how you see yourself. Go ahead write in the book! Date your personal impressions and then come back 365 days from now and check out your accuracy.

If you want to have some fun with this exercise, share your list with your spouse or someone who knows you very well. Step one, see if your partner generally agrees with the words you recorded. You could well discover your partner has two or three additional ideas for your consideration and contemplation.

Step two, as you may have surmised, is to see how they honestly and brutally rate you on the scale of one to ten. As a cautionary note, never ask your parents or your favourite aunt to do this. Scoring a perfect ten is great for the ego, but it is not too practical. When the ratings are at great variance to your own, don't forget to ask why.

All you are attempting here is to get some sense of how you mesh with what is perceived to be important from a client standpoint. I would have to confess that my score under the flexibility heading would have been abysmally low. What do you expect? I was a banker for twenty-five years! To be successful in the re-employment consulting business, I had to develop a radical new mind-set when it came to flexibility.

If you have been forthright and honest in this evaluation, you will likely discover you have three or four areas where you, too, are going to need to make a conscious effort to change. In fact, as you have an opportunity to complete more research while preparing to start up your business, you should revisit this list to make any necessary changes to the top ten items.

What are my Self-Enhancement Goals?

Your next challenge is to map out an action plan. Remember, no one is going to do this for you. We are back to the now well worn reality of being both employer and employee.

Deep down, most of us know our own shortcomings. Even if we readily acknowledge our main deficiencies, human nature often conspires against us, and we procrastinate about taking action to eliminate or minimize our limitations. If you have come from a corporate background, good employers will have assisted you in identifying areas for improvement. In many cases, the employer will have also supplied the training vehicles to address those soft spots requiring attention.

Now that you are your own employer, this task falls squarely upon your shoulders, including finding the time and the financial resources to rectify matters. Self-imposed goal setting for self-enhancement is an absolute must when you are on your own.

If you have a reasonable sense about where you need to help yourself, jot down the three major items in your Day Timer, but make the notation one month from today. No, I am not aiding and abetting your tendency to procrastinate. Over the course of the next thirty days you will be inundated with information derived from your research. As a result of this research and your general observations, you might well discover your self-enhancement priorities have changed. Once you have focused on the top three priorities, take the necessary action to get started and systematically spread out your learning endeavours over the next twelve months.

If I could hazard a guess about the two areas where most of us need some refinement, I would pinpoint written communications and presentation skills. These two subjects will crop up in other chapters. Why? Number one, written communication, is vital. Getting your message across in a clear and concise fashion will set you apart from your competitors.

Number two, presentation skills, will prove invaluable as you build and expand your consulting business. Think back to your impressions about consultants you have dealt with in the past. The memorable ones are likely those who were able to communicate with ease and who presented their services and products in a professional manner.

When you take your next break, wander over to your nearest bookstore and purchase a copy of Peter Urs Bender's book entitled *Secrets of Power Presentations.* It will become your second most important book as you prepare to venture into your own business.

This chapter is intended to provoke some careful thought so you can achieve a well defined personal focus. Circumstances can cause today's crystal clear focus to become fuzzy. With that in mind, you should periodically re-evaluate what you want and your review should coincide with your annual business assessment — the company year end. What better time to reflect on the past twelve months, to adjust your personal and business objectives and to prepare for an upcoming year.

CHAPTER 3

Focus — Getting to Know My Company

Chapter three marks the beginning of the fun part of starting up your own consulting firm. Don't be misled. Just because this is often seen as the creative segment it is very serious business since you are beginning to shape the image your clients will associate with you and your company name. The decisions you make concerning items covered in the next several pages are meant to be revisited frequently before you arrive at any final conclusions.

Perhaps the best way to assist you in developing an image is to pose some of the questions my corporate clients were never shy about asking. Going through this process will benefit you in two ways. One, you start to anticipate what clients want to know, and two, you learn how to weave together what they want with what you can offer.

Jot down your initial responses to these questions, and you will begin to see an image emerging. Don't worry if that image is a bit hazy at the moment. How your company will look to the buyer of your services and products will slowly crystalize.

What does your company do? Have you a speciality?

The question seems simple. Unfortunately, many a new consultant has blown a good prospect meeting by not being able to answer clearly. Write down, in point form, everything you believe your company can do and can deliver. Keep coming back to the list with the intention of refining it to one or two sentences. In due course, reciting your reply should be as natural as giving your name and address.

What you do should not be confused with how you do it. How you do it is your mission statement. I have a phobia about mission statements, I think because so many large firms point with pride to a smoothly crafted series of words that supposedly represents how they do business. But as you get to know some of those organizations you find what they say is not necessarily what they do. Be extremely carefully when penning your own mission statement.

What sets your company apart from your competitors? Why would someone utilize your firm instead of your competitors?

This question implies you have taken the time to research your competitors. If you haven't, don't drop this book and head out the door. However, I would urge you to accumulate data about those companies that will be vying for the assignments you want. And don't stop at companies the same size as your own. You will want to have a good handle on competitors two or three rungs above you. Remember, just because you are small does not necessarily mean you can't compete with larger firms.

What sets you apart from others? Go back and read those descriptive words we discussed in the previous section. I am not suggesting you memorize a list of adverbs and adjectives simply to impress a potential client. You need to focus on three or four, which you truly believe in.

Let me give you a quick personal example. When I was in the re-employment counselling business I always emphasized that I was accessible at any time. I had a direct-line phone number on my business card and all my printed material. I knew being reachable was a key selling point. I promised clients they could track me down twenty-four hours a day and I would get back to them within three hours. That feature was one of a handful that constantly set me apart from big and small competitors.

Are there limitations to the size of contract you can handle?

This is a loaded question that requires careful consideration. The reason for raising it now is to get you thinking about the parameters of your business. It may also cause you to give some thought to issues like establishing contingency plans by being able to call upon others in your field, should a need arise.

In my experience, clients invariably appreciate an honest answer. The forthright approach is much more likely to endear you to a client who will make a mental note to consider you for a chance at a smaller assignment in the future. That assumes you have not attempted to mislead the person during initial discussions.

Do you concentrate on a specific geographic area?

Your response will depend on a number of factors, including the type of business you are involved in and your personal viewpoints on travel. Sometimes it is wise to acquire more information before you answer. You might be inclined to say no to a one-week contract on the other side of the country, but what if a client wanted you to spend six months on an assignment? I used to say I was very flexible depending on the circumstances.

Tell me about the background of your company and the other professionals who work there. How long have you been in business?

Another loaded question, particularly if you have only been in business for a whole two weeks. It's good to tie your previous work experience to your new business. Indeed, it is one of the reasons professional profiles of business owners are included in company literature. Such a profile tells a client your qualifications and, by extension, why your company can do the work.

In cases where you have been doing consulting work on the side, you can mention this to offset any negatives that might be associated with your company's youth. One of my former clients had worked weekends for several years selling and servicing computers. When he decided to move into full-time office computer consulting he could easily explain the transition.

If we asked you to handle an assignment, who would actually do the work?

Be honest. It is preferable to be able to say you will be handling the assignment, particularly if it is the first contract.

One of the biggest advantages of a small independent consulting practise is that paying clients are working with the owner. There can be some downside risk to the purchaser of services if you get hit by a Mac truck halfway through the assignment. That said, I truly believe representatives of larger firms like dealing with smaller businesses when it is workable. Good independent consultants are often viewed as more responsive because so much depends on completing a project in a fully satisfactory fashion. Remember, you are only as good as the results of your last assignment.

When considering potential new suppliers we like to make some reference checks. Can you provide me with references?

This matter warrants careful consideration. If you are brand new and have never had a real contract before, you will need to rely on your personal reputation. Give some thought to those old associates who would endorse your personal abilities.

You might select a previous boss or peer who would be willing to extol your virtues. Or you might recall someone from the past who moved into consulting before you did. I have found the latter group to be an excellent source for general references, since they have a good understanding of how tough it can be to get a new business up and running.

Whatever you do, don't spring these situations on any of your potential references. Take the time to drop by and see them to explain your new business. Then they'll know exactly what you are attempting to do. And who knows? They might be able to give you some pointers. Come to think of it, your references are often your first real networking contacts.

In the past I have made a concerted effort to get to know my fellow consultants, even if they might be seen as competitors. I have found there is a certain bond amongst consultants, I think because we have all taken the plunge into self-employment. You never know when you might need to rely on someone else for support.

Can you send me a copy of your literature?

Unless you are extraordinary well focused, it is doubtful your first information package will be 100% complete. On the other hand, you don't want to be making too many changes in the first year. I would suggest a compromise. Develop a comprehensive information kit that you can use for six to twelve months, but acknowledge to yourself that this is likely to need a review before you produce any material for the long term. We will revisit this issue in one of the following chapters.

I'm not familiar with the area around your office address. Exactly where are you located?

Loaded question number three. I don't know too many first-time consultants who charge out and sign a five-year lease in an office complex. Frankly I would recommend you not do this until you have a much better understanding about your office requirements. Many of us start out working from home or from an executive centre. For now, honesty is the best policy.

If you are working from home and there is no need for you to have a fancy office, say so. I often joked with people that my real office was my car. I would go on to say that in my line of business, most of my time was spent at client locations. Office facilities were an unnecessary luxury, particularly in these technologically advanced days when I was in constant touch with my home base via phone and e-mail. Even the more skeptical types can be won over if you are efficient and respond to them in a timely fashion.

The information in the last two chapters is meant to act as a catalyst, to stimulate your thought processes. By now you should have a better impression of your personal goals. You should also be getting to know a little more about this entity called your company. Armed with that information, you are now ready to turn your attention to some of the organizational aspects associated with starting up your business.

CHAPTER 4

Organization
Practical Planning — Business Details

Getting to know your company is not an eight-hour exercise accomplished by answering the questions posed in the last chapter. To prepare for the launch of your company, you will find you are constantly refining and fine tuning a host of details.

Now might be a good time to temporarily shift gears and begin to consider the more practical issues. All too often, I have seen excellent, well-qualified consultants make major mistakes by not seeking out professional assistance from the outset. Those who have fallen into this trap were convinced they were too small to start worrying about tax implications, financial planning and sundry odd legal matters. Some wanted to save a buck by doing it themselves. Don't take any shortcuts when it comes to assembling your experts.

Let me be clear on who falls in this expert category. Included on the roster will be a: banker, lawyer, accountant, financial planner, life insurance agent, property insurance broker, printer/graphic designer and perhaps other specialists depending on your type of business. Certainly these seven are a must for most new businesses.

Remember, you will have an ongoing, long-term relationship with most or all of your support team. It only makes sense to select those who are:

- competent and responsive
- knowledgeable about consulting businesses
- interested in dealing with your size of company
- personally a good fit with you and any partners you may have

Finding the right professionals can be a tall order. Don't assume the lawyer you used for your last mortgage or will is necessarily the person you want to have as a legal advisor for your company. Maybe he or she only does mortgages and wills and has not kept pace with the ever-changing legal requirements relating to business practices. The same might apply to the neighbourhood accountant who has competently prepared your personal tax return for the past eight years.

So how do you go about finding and selecting your support team? Most of us have had occasion to use an accountant or a lawyer. If you have been completely satisfied with the work they have done in the past, they at least deserve the opportunity to bid for your company account.

Phone them, briefly explain what you are contemplating and then arrange for a formal meeting. You want to see them in person to discuss your plans and gauge their responses to your queries. During the meeting you want to discover:

- if they handle your type of business
- what assistance they can offer in the start-up phase
- who would handle your account
- what they would require from you if they were chosen
- a general idea about fees

If the answer to the first question is no, you at least have a chance to ask for other recommendations. If the responses to the other questions are vague or noncommittal, look elsewhere for help. Trust me when I say investing time in deciding upon the right professional help at the outset is essential.

You don't want to be changing accountants after three years because you find your accountants are so busy concentrating on personal tax returns in March and April that they fail to reply to your business inquiries. There is also some truth to the old saying that you get what you pay for. I always look at the fees charged by my team as an investment and not as an expense. Obviously I am not sending copies of this book to any of them!

Should you have no idea who to contact, start making some calls to relatives, friends and business associates. Explain what type of help you are looking for. Your brother-in-law may have a fantastic accounting firm to suggest, but if they only deal with mega corporations, you might not be happy with the service. On the other hand, your brother-in-law's personal acquaintance at a huge accounting firm might be happy to put you in touch with an old colleague who specializes in small business accounting.

Once you have a few names, start interviewing. Your spouse might have some involvement with your company. You had both better be comfortable with the professional help you select. My wife, the novice legal wizard in the family, could not tolerate our first lawyer. You guessed it — we now have a new lawyer we are both happy to deal with. And he was recommended by our previous partners, whose judgement we trusted implicitly.

In the upcoming few pages, I will offer some insight concerning who handles what, accompanied by a few cautionary notes.

ACCOUNTANTS

There is no particular reason for starting with the accountant, other than to emphasize the new breed of bean counter need not fit the stereotype of twenty or thirty years ago. Yes, they must still be accurate, detail oriented and relatively cautious, but they also have to exhibit some business sense.

My accountant is Barry Watson, of Watson Dauphinee & Masuch in Vancouver. You might think that is a plug for Barry's firm, but it isn't — I do have a point or two to make. When I got into the consulting game in Vancouver, I was searching for a knowledgeable accountant who understood people in the consulting business. I also wanted to deal with one of the partners of the firm and not a junior employee who could be here today and gone tomorrow.

Egotistical? Maybe, but I work hard for my money and I want to know who I am dealing with. Barry fit the bill perfectly. He came with the added plus of being endorsed by my brother-in-law, who is also an independent consultant. Now you may think the foregoing is just so much rambling on my part but if you want to increase your chances for success, you need to find an accountant you can relate to.

Once you've chosen, what's the next step? Don't forget, you are paying this person for advice and guidance. During the first real meeting — the one where the fee clock is ticking — I'd be asking for input and direction on the topics listed below. The only documents I would send to the accountant's office before the meeting are a detailed personal financial statement and a personal expense summary. You will want to bring your financial and business planning notes to the first meeting, but remember, this is a planning session. Trust me, you'll be back for more visits.

Cash Flow Projections /
Projected Income & Expense Statement

In the simplest of accounting terms (personally I can only handle single-syllable accounting jargon) a cash flow projection is an over-view for the upcoming twelve months which records your revenue estimates and then deducts anticipated operating costs and other expenses. These figures generally come from your projected income and expense statement. The projection will show you where and when you will have negative and positive cash flow. Negative is when you will need to borrow or inject other sources of cash; positive is when the company is self-sufficient. Early on in your discussions, your accountant will also establish an opening balance sheet for your company.

To develop a good cash flow projection, your accountant is going to want you to meticulously lay out all your expenses, including your salary or draw. You will need to estimate when and how much revenue you will generate.

Most of us quickly learn the expression "negative cash flow." That sometimes frightening figure is most evident during the start-up months and often equates to the amount of personal equity you need to inject into the company to get things up and running. Many of your larger initial expenditures (computers, other equipment, office furniture, office improvement and so on) contribute to this negative cash flow in the first few months. It does not matter if these items are eventually expensed or capitalized. You still need to find the money to make the purchases, and I can almost guarantee your friendly banker will want to see a cash flow projection if you intend to borrow.

Your Professional Fee Structure

During your discussions about anticipated revenues, the subject of your fee structure will undoubtedly need to be addressed. Most consultants are faced with having to be able to quote in at least three different ways — hourly, daily and by the project.

While there are several formulas you can use to set hourly or daily fees, the primary influencing factor is the marketplace itself. Formulas and gut reactions might suggest you are worth $150 per hour, but if all your qualified competitors are charging $100 to $125, you are in for an uphill struggle. My advice is to know precisely what your competitors charge. Then massage your projections accordingly and realistically.

Truth be told, the rate is only a small part of the equation. Billable time is the key factor. In other words, how many billable hours or days do you have to work in a year to generate enough income to cover all expenses (including your own draw) and still be left with a profit. Don't forget the profit part! That is your annual reward for being an entrepreneurial risk taker. Besides, profits allow you to build and expand your business.

If you are involved in project work, you could well be faced with additional variables when setting contract fees for an entire undertaking. In these scenarios your hourly or per diem rates will come into play, but you will also have to be cognizant of other associated expenses. These could include: travel, travel time, extra equipment, additional professional or clerical support, materials, postage, courier fees and printed material.

When you quote on a project, include all your expenses in one fashion or another. In some situations you may increase the total cost of the project; in other cases you might base your quote on a set fee, with specified expenses to be covered by the client.

When all is said and done, your fees must be competitive and justifiable to your clients. Remember, even if you establish a fair and sensible fee structure, the bigger challenge is to secure the work!

Accounting Procedures and Systems

Accounting procedures vary greatly depending on circumstances. One major influencing factor is whether you are incorporated. You and your accountant will need to decide the extent of your involvement in areas such as record keeping, bookkeeping and financial administration.

The rule of thumb is the more you do (correctly), the smaller your accounting bill will be. Wide variances can occur. On one hand, you can write the cheques, calculate and file your GST, issue the invoices, make the bank deposits and maintain all the associated records in neat order. Your accountant will still have a fairly significant job to do prior to your year end, as he or she will be preparing your books. If you go this route, make certain you clearly understand all your responsibilities.

If you want to move to the next level, you can purchase an accounting package for your computer and faithfully make all the necessary entries. By the way, your accountant can offer some advice about which program to buy, so your software will be consistent with the accounting firm. Let me add an important cautionary note on this subject. If you are not mentally equipped (as I am not) or generally inclined (as I am not) to handle this administrative task, don't!

Your accountant will be more than happy to relay some horror stories about first-time business owners who come to their accountants after six months, begging to be relieved of the bookkeeping. Get it right from the start! Remember, your objective is to be out there making money, not tearing your hair out over a computer program you cannot master.

Tax Payments

There are numerous ways to handle tax payments, and your accountant will guide you through the necessary procedures. Whatever you do, you don't want to fall into the trap of treating your revenue as net income. If you do, you might encounter an enormous and disconcerting financial revelation when your personal and company taxes come due.

Incorporation Versus Sole Ownership/Partnership

Your decision on this subject will be driven by type of business and input from your accountant and lawyer. The need or advisability to limit personal liability usually plays a major role in deciding whether to incorporate. Also, your anticipated revenues can influence if and when you should incorporate, as there are tax implications to be considered.

If personal liability issues are minor, you may find that your accountant and lawyer suggest starting off as a sole ownership or partnership. However, if you go this route, keep your accountant plugged in when your revenues accelerate quickly. Reaching certain revenue thresholds will necessitate a re-evaluation of the merits of incorporating.

If you decide to incorporate now or at some point in the future, you will want to discuss the selection of the most advantageous year end for your company. Choosing the right year end may allow you to take advantage of some temporary tax deferrals. As well, when you incorporate, your accountant and lawyer will decide how to structure the share distribution in the company. (Should you eventually decide to sell your company, proper share structuring can have tax implications.)

At the end of the day, don't forget the true cost of incorporating is not just the fee charged to establish a limited company. As soon as you incorporate you are faced with more complex reporting to government agencies, and accounting procedures become more time consuming and therefore more expensive.

Leasing Versus Borrowing

Another true confession from the author: I have yet to determine when it is advantageous to lease and when it is more beneficial to take out a term loan to finance major capital expenditures. Everyone you talk to will have an opinion on the subject.

Either form of financing will assist you in spreading the impact of a purchase over time, and that can be a big bonus when it comes to keeping your cash flow in the positive column. If you listen to some pundits, it is easier to get a lease than to arrange a bank loan. I believe there could be some validity to that argument, given that leasing companies have mechanisms in place to more easily take a charge over the equipment you are acquiring.

Any financial expert will tell you not to draw on your operating line of credit to finance major capital expenditures. Be guided by your team of professionals. Talk to your accountant before you make any major financial commitments.

Sundry Accounting Issues

You will also want to ask your accountant about GST registration, GST payments and what business expenses can be legitimately written off — home office, vehicles, entertainment, memberships, gifts, conventions and the like.

Ask your accountant! Don't be guided by comments from well-intentioned friends and business associates. When you talk to your accountant, clarify exactly what record keeping responsibilities rest on your shoulders. You don't want to be reconstructing your business mileage records from three years ago when Revenue Canada asks for documentation to back up your claims.

Unless you have a natural inclination toward financial matters, you should be thoroughly confused by the time you conclude your first meeting with the accountant. Be patient. The confusion could escalate as soon as you see your lawyer.

LAWYER

To be consistent with the scenario I just painted about my account-ant, it only seems fair to give you the same background regarding my lawyer. Even more so given my earlier comments about changing lawyers. Okay, I confess. I committed the unthinkable sin of origi-nally selecting a lawyer for my business based on his proficiency as a mortgage lawyer. I did say I would share my mistakes with you!

My lawyer today is Bob Crouch of Prouse, Dash & Crouch in Brampton, Ontario. As I said, he was referred by two old business associates. Bob is not inexpensive but he invariably keeps me on side. What's more, he is accessible and he has a sense of urgency when matters require immediate action. I say all those kind words not to swell Bob's head, but to give you an understanding of what is important to a small business person like myself and yourself.

Your lawyer is part of your team, and he or she must be able to work with your accountant. The overlaps between legal counsel and accounting advice are increasing at a rapid pace. The two had better be able to work in concert without individual egos getting in the way of your business goals.

And what do you want to review with your lawyer? Consider some of the following agenda items for your first formal meeting:

Incorporation Versus Not

The decision to incorporate is usually influenced by both legal and financial considerations. Your lawyer will be in the best position to explain the personal liability issues.

Numbered Companies

Most business lawyers maintain a few pre-registered numbered companies on the shelf, as it were. Incorporating a company can be done almost instantly by using a numbered company. You can always alter the name of the company later, and the change is not an onerous task. Or you can simply retain the number company and register a trade name or names as needed.

Bank Signing Authorities

Whether you opt for sole ownership, partnership or limited company, you will want to discuss the issue of bank signing authorities with your lawyer. In most cases, your decisions will hinge on convenience, adequate protection and what might happen if you are incapacitated, or in the event of your untimely demise. Have your lawyer explain all the implications so you can make an informed choice.

Contracts

Depending upon your business, you might be faced with some complicated contracts between yourself (your company) and your clients. While it may not be appropriate to have your lawyer immediately leap into preparing documents, you will want to offer an overview of your requirements. By having these preliminary conversations on day one, your lawyer will be in a better position to respond much more quickly when a need arises.

Partnership Agreements

If the establishment of your consulting firm involves a partnership arrangement, this matter will require the utmost care and attention. Many partnerships have ended in divorce because a proper and comprehensive partnership agreement was not negotiated and signed at the outset of the marriage. Worse still, some partners try to save a few bucks and design their own partnership contract. The consequences are about the same as you defending yourself in a divorce action.

If something as seemingly sacred as a marriage between two people is subject to dissolution, why would you think for a moment that the same thing could not happen in a business partnership? As one lawyer put it, signing a "pre-nup" agreement with a business partner is more important than signing one with an intended spouse.

At this very instant, half of my readers are thinking these words of wisdom do not apply to them. I can offer only one comment. Good luck! I am confident your lawyer will endorse my sentiments. Spending the money to have a proper partnership agreement prepared will be one of your wisest investments. Take it from someone who knows. The same cautionary note applies to working arrangements in an incorporated entity where you are not the only shareholder.

Personal Wills

If you are embarking on a major change in your business life, it is only sensible and practical to revisit your personal will(s). As an independent consultant, you have increased responsibilities to protect your family. Make certain your will is redrawn to reflect all the changes in your life.

I am frequently asked for my opinion in terms of what makes a new business successful. The question does not have an easy answer, but I will say having and using a good lawyer will enhance your chances immensely.

FINANCIAL PLANNERS / INVESTMENT BROKERS

The uninitiated often ask, "Why do I need a financial planner and/or an investment broker if I already have an accountant?" After years of asking the same question, I finally have the answer. Accountants tell you what you need to do from an income tax perspective, and financial planners / investment brokers help you make the right decisions about how to do it.

Look at it another way. When you eventually arrive at the enviable plateau where you have more income than expenses, it is not going to be your accountant who tells you where to invest the surplus funds. Your accountant will be able to confirm that you are in a position to invest, but in my mind, an accountant is not necessarily qualified to tell you where. Similarly, I would not rely on my accountant to recommend how to diversify my RSP portfolio, or how to maximize yields from a positive cash flow.

In passing let me acknowledge Lynn Biscott, Sid Smith and Ed Yablonski. I am an author and a consultant in human resources and marketing — I am not a financial planner. Like my accountant and my lawyer, these three people are experts in their own fields.

Surround yourself with true professionals and be guided by their input. Start now. And don't ask your team of professionals to make your decisions for you. They are hired to provide you with quality information and logical options. Remember, when you are on your own, the buck stops at your own doorstep.

BANKERS

Attempting to establish a long-term working relationship with your banker is a task not easily accomplished. Unlike other members of your team of professionals, the banker will change from time to time, simply because banks often transfer employees. And not all bank branches are mandated to deal with small business loans.

Drop by your existing branch and set up an appointment with an appropriate person. Emphasize you simply want to have an informal discussion concerning your upcoming plans to open a consulting business.

During the first meeting, you will want to offer your banker a brief overview of your plans. Confirm whether the branch handles small business accounts, including loan accommodations.

Even if you don't think you will need any financing, you are going to want to establish a sound working relationship with a branch that can offer loan assistance. There is nothing more perplexing than being faced with a need for a loan, only to find you are being asked to review your requirements with a total stranger at another office.

Should you need a term loan for capital expenditures, or operating assistance to finance receivables, do not get involved in discussions with your banker until you are prepared with the facts and figures.

If after further discussions with your accountant and lawyer you decide a lending facility is needed, phone your banker to see what paperwork they want from you. Personal financial statements will be at the top of their list, followed quickly by cash flow estimates. Depending on the amounts involved, you might be asked for a formal business plan. (The business plan will be covered in Chapter 16, after you have reviewed all the aspects of starting and marketing your own business.)

If you are borrowing money, your banker's major concerns are going to be how you will repay the debt and when. Your banker will likely be looking for two sources of repayment. The primary one could be your receivables, but bankers like to have a backup plan. Those contingency plans include personal guarantees (if you are borrowing under the name of a limited company) and perhaps a charge against one or more of your assets. Collateral may include stock or the equity in your personal residence.

I have had more than my fair share of conversations with deflated entrepreneurs after they have come from seeing their banker. In most cases the root cause of the problem is a lack of preparation by the would-be borrower.

In defence of the bankers, they do have a tough job. If you want a sound working relationship with your banker, remember two important items. Keep them informed and provide them with the thoroughly prepared detail material and data they request.

LIFE INSURANCE AGENTS

If your past life included working for a reasonably large employer, you likely were afforded a number of benefits. Those may have included life insurance, accident insurance, disability insurance, medical insurance, dental and eyeglass coverage and so on. Most employees take benefits for granted. As a self-employed businessperson you are about to discover the true value and the cost of benefits.

I don't know about you, but the mention of an insurance agent can cause me to twitch uncontrollably, immediately followed by a vision of unrelenting high-pressure sales calls. What you need is an insurance consultant who is able to listen to your situation, assimilate the information and then put forward a professional proposal, complete with options. Fortunately for me, I found Virginia Maloney, who researches and consults before she sells.

This book is not going to tell you whether you need whole life, term life, disability insurance, mortgage insurance or whatever. Why? Because each situation is unique and personal. I would caution that you are not simply purchasing insurance products to replace those you may have had with a previous employer. Now that you're self-employed you need alternate or supplementary protection for you and your family. The most notable example is work-interruption or disability protection.

Insurance can also affect your estate and retirement planning. To further complicate matters, you also have to deal with the reality of affordability. A good insurance agent will to put together a sensible and understandable package that addresses your immediate and longer term needs.

You don't want a good insurance agent, you want a great one. Make a few phone calls to your self-employed friends and relatives. I suspect you will encounter someone who can offer a name and a solution.

INSURANCE BROKERS

Nearly all of us have insurance on vehicles, homes and contents. If we are lucky, we never have occasion to find out if the broker and the insurance company are any good. If you have lived through a nightmare claim experience, you will have an appreciation of just how important it is to have a good broker, backed up by a competent insurance company.

Like everyone else on your professional team, you need to find a dependable broker. Then you need to explain your new business. Your insurance requirements will vary greatly depending upon where your office is situated — at home, in an executive office suite or in leased premises.

Coverage for vehicles and equipment used in your business also deserves close scrutiny. Liability coverage might also come into play. You don't want any surprises if someone slips in your driveway while on the way to see you in your home office above the garage!

Your prime concern should be to have adequate insurance. Align yourself with an insurance firm known to expedite claims should they occur. Charging around town getting quotes for a stolen computer is not something you want to bother with when you are in the midst of a major assignment.

Like everything else in setting up your own business, thorough investigation concerning property and liability insurance coverage will save you time and money.

PRINTERS AND GRAPHIC ARTISTS

You may find it odd that I have included a printer as part of your professional support team. Never overlook the pros who make you look good! All consultants will need letterhead, business cards and envelopes. Many of us will require brochures, forms, contracts, agreements and other advertising material.

In upcoming chapters, I will discuss many of these items as they pertain to the image you wish to create for your company. At this juncture I simply want to plant the seed in your mind about a printer. While you are making those phone calls to get some suggestions for a good accountant or a great insurance agent, you might also want to pose a question or two about reputable printers and artists.

I would seek out an owner-operated printing shop. Unless you have a printing background, don't tell your printers what you want. Give them some general ideas and let them make some suggestions. Once you nail down precisely what you want, get at least three quotes. Price isn't everything when it comes to printing, but you can find some significant variations.

When you come right down to it, printers are a temperamental lot. It must have something to do with their creative genes. Ivan Pomakov, my Minuteman Press owner, falls in this category. But, after dealing with him for ten years, I know I am going to receive a high quality product which is delivered on time and at a fair price. He is also going to tell me when I am doing something stupid. That is the kind of person I want on my consulting team.

Depending on the nature of your business, your list of professionals may be longer. Take time in selecting those people who will help you grow your company. And remember: you do get what you pay for!

CHAPTER 5

Organization
Practical Planning — Office and Equipment

Decisions about your office and equipment will be vital to effectively starting up your own consulting practice. For many of us who have never been involved in such an undertaking, the experience can be daunting but fun nonetheless.

There are two words you must keep in mind during this process — flexible and expandable. Because you have no track record, you can only estimate your future requirements.

OFFICE SPACE

Selecting the right office space and the right location needs a great deal of consideration. There are innumerable factors to weigh. Some of those may relate to your personal preferences — don't forget, this is your own company. Others will be tightly linked to outside forces, like client expectations and perceptions.

Let me pose a few questions to help you achieve an overview of items that need to be considered. Then I will supply you with some observations to assist you in your decision-making.

Where are my prospective clients located? Where do I intend to concentrate my long-term marketing efforts?

Proximity to your clients is not necessarily a must, depending on the type of consulting work you do. On the other hand, if you are involved in consulting to a very specific industry and generally those companies are concentrated in one area of the city, you want to bring this factor into your deliberations. The same might also hold true if you were convinced you were only going to focus on potential clients within a certain geographic area.

Given the services I provide, will clients be coming to see me? Are such visits likely to be regular or rare? Does my office need to be conveniently located?

If you anticipate that clients will be coming to see you regularly, accessibility will be a major item to consider. Indeed, the answer to the above question could well determine if you will seek leased space or executive office facilities.

In the event your type of consulting business invariably goes to the client location, you have some other options, including a home office setup.

What do my competitors use for office facilities?

You need not be restricted by what your competitors do, but it is a good idea to know about their facilities and where they are located. In the past, some of my clients would ask why I didn't have a splashy office in the middle of the city. My answer was that I was always in their office if I was on assignment. I took pride in the fact I was frugal when it came to unnecessary trappings. But I made a point of casually letting my clients know that my home office would rival any leading office facility.

It is interesting to note many of my business associates quickly sought me out when their companies started encouraging people to work from home.

When I have a contract or an assignment, am I more likely to be working out of my office, or will I be on-site at my client's location?

If you spend a great deal of your time at a customer's site and you do not meet with them at your office, you instantly have many more options when it comes to your own office location.

On day one, how much space do I need for myself, support personnel and storage?

If you start up your business as a one-person operation, life is simple. As soon as you need to bring others on board to provide support or assistance, you are faced with changing circumstances. Don't overlook the storage issue, either. Again, this will depend on your type of business.

My existing businesses are run from a 7 by 12 foot home office, albeit with the added luxury of an extra storage locker in the basement of our apartment condo. Could I effectively run the operation in this location if I needed a full-time support person? The answer is no.

If I go the home office route to start, what are the business and family implications? Also, where would the home office be situated? What would be the cost of any premises improvements?

If your spouse works away from home all day and the kids are all in high school or at college, a home office might be quite plausible.

In the event you have a large home but you have three youngsters, all under the age of six, a home office might work, but you will want to define some boundaries and decide upon a few basic rules.

A home office can be an inexpensive alternative. I would, however, encourage you to treat the office space as a business place. Spend the money to transform it to business status.

If I look at an executive suite or a lease, what are the implications?

I am a big fan of the executive office facility if it is impractical to work out of your own home. Monthly rental fees vary greatly and depend on the size of the office, the location, the duration of rental arrangement and the services included with the rental contract. Normally you also have the flexibility of acquiring additional space should your business volumes so dictate.

A few of my friends have winced at the rental payments, which are naturally higher than if you went out and leased space. Don't forget, part of what you are paying for is peace of mind and not having a long-term lease. Often you also benefit from having access (usually at a price) to other services and facilities such as: a boardroom, a kitchen, telephone answering, couriers, mail handling and even typing.

Your decision should hinge on what you need to service your prospective clients and what fits into your initial start-up plans. Above all else, keep things flexible so you can expand with relative ease.

EQUIPMENT / FURNISHINGS

Naturally your equipment and furniture requirements are going to be driven in large measure by your selection of office facilities. For the sake of this discussion I am going to assume it is practical and makes good business sense for you to start your venture in a home office setting. Please don't assume I am necessarily recommending this course of action.

Desks, Credenzas, Filing Cabinets, Chairs and Workstations

The first two criteria for selecting furniture are personal comfort and practicality. It really doesn't matter if your preference is a formal arrangement like someone's big corner office or if you are more at ease with a very functional layout like many of the modern workstation formats.

As I have said to many of my colleagues who have switched to home office work environments, the key thing to remember is that you are going to be spending a great deal of time in your office, and it should be what you want. Practicality does come into play in terms of limitations like physical size and your budget.

Don't necessarily assume that you should utilize your existing den furniture. Take the time to visit a few office furniture suppliers and get a sense of what is available. If you do opt for new furniture, go with the highest quality product you can afford, and if possible, select an open stock model. If your business is booming a year down the road and you need to expand into leased premises, it can be annoying to discover you can't find furniture to match what you have already purchased.

Almost every consultant I know has thrown out his or her first filing cabinet. They all look the same, but it is what is inside that counts. This is one item where you will want to spend the money to go with a top-of-the-line model, and it will give you years of service. If you can't afford a first-class new one, look in used office supply stores.

Chairs tend to fall in the same category as filing cabinets. Without doubt, the most important chair in the office is the one you sit on. It is worthwhile to spend a few dollars more on your desk chair and economize on client chairs.

Computer Systems

For those of you who use a computer as an integral part of your consulting practice, you can probably skip this section. For the rest of you, those who require a computer for correspondence, accounting, record keeping and a diary system, here are some tips — learned the hard way, I might add.

If your existing computer is more than two years old, I strongly suspect you will need to invest in a new one. The old model may handle your day-to-day home needs, but as soon as you start loading the more complex office-related software, you are going to run into a capacity problem. You are going to want a computer with a modem to handle e-mail, faxes and access to the Internet.

I am not advocating that you spend a fortune on a general-use computer system. But you do need to be technically up to date. Look for a system that has the flexibility to expand. Just to add a little more confusion, do you go with a lap top or a desk model? The decision comes down to three items: personal preference, need for a travelling companion and cost.

When it comes to a monitor, I would again suggest you select the biggest and best you can afford. With any luck, a good quality monitor might outlast two or three CPUs.

Turning to printers, the rules are simple. If you have a dot matrix printer, give it away now. At a bare minimum you will need a high quality desk jet but for the difference in price, I would go with a laser from the very start. Depending on your type of business, a colour printer may have merit, particularly if you will be doing a number of presentations.

Invest in a label maker capable of producing individual mailing labels. They are relatively inexpensive and they make your large envelopes look professionally prepared.

Computer Software

Honestly I don't know if WordPerfect is better than Microsoft Word. I do know that many of my consulting colleagues spend a great deal of time hammering away on their keyboards. With that in mind, your personal preference or your comfort level should generally determine what software you purchase. However, in some cases, software and even hardware choices could be influenced by what is traditionally used by your clients.

Two types of software deserve a little extra attention. If you think you will be making presentations requiring overheads and if you have not used this type of software in the past, take some time to research two or three of the big names. Your two primary criteria will be ease of use and end results.

The second type of program, and I think this is the most important purchase, is a data base for maintaining client information. Let me digress for a moment in an effort to save you some time. If you are going to mount an effective marketing and networking attack, it is absolutely imperative you immediately start using some form of client tracking system.

The one I have found to be the most flexible and adaptable is something called Maximizer, but there are several similar products on the market today. At a minimum, you will want a program that can handle the following functions:

- storage of contact names, addresses and phone numbers
- automatic diary system
- label and envelope printing
- mail merge for correspondence
- word processing and correspondence storage
- note section for client write-ups
- search capability by company, contact name, and so on
- automatic fax dialling

As soon as you get the software installed, start loading in every shred of information off every business card you have. Whenever you meet someone new, get in the habit of immediately inputting their data when you get to the office.

Why am I so adamant about this? Well, one of the most common complaints I hear from consultants is that they don't have enough time to do their marketing. Trust me. If you use one of these systems faithfully, your marketing efforts will be infinitely easier and you will be able to keep ahead of your correspondence.

Oh, by the way, another true confession. I waited three years before I bought my Maximizer system and I wouldn't wish converting a thousand client files on my worst enemy. Maybe you can convince some unsuspecting teen in your household to begin keyboarding tonight!

Fax Machines

Whoever invented the plain paper fax machine deserves a few accolades. A high quality plain paper fax / printer / scanner / mini copier is a good choice for many office situations. Even if you do not intend to use the equipment as your primary printer, I would definitely go with a plain paper model. Over and above the convenience of using ordinary paper, they are easy to operate and they have a workable amount of memory.

If you select the executive office route, you might find it is more practical to have your own fax in your private office. One factor to consider is the degree of confidentiality associated with your work and the other issue relates purely to accessibility.

Phone Systems

If you are running your consulting business from home, you need to have additional phone lines installed, one for your company phone and another for the fax and modem. Do not try to get by with the family phone line(s). Sort out the phone situation before you move forward with printing letterhead and business cards.

Whatever you do, have a dedicated fax line, assuming you want to present a professional image. There is nothing more exasperating than reaching voice mail on what you thought was a fax line. To me, this instantly conveys the wrong image.

Here is a trick of the trade: list your cell phone number as your direct line. When you are not in your car, simply forward it to your home office. You will achieve two things. One, you are much more accessible to your clients. Two, if you do eventually have to relocate offices, clients can still reach you at the same direct line number. I have been in three office locations in the past seven years, and throughout the changes, my clients have always been able to reach me — even on moving days.

You are going to need a quality phone with speed dial and a speaker phone option. Voice mail, preferably through the phone company, is a must. Remember, most people are not opposed to leaving a message but they do become irate when the person does not respond quickly.

Handling your phone requirements in the manner outlined above is easy and cost efficient. There is one drawback: most phone companies will not include a company listing in the phone book if you don't pay for a commercial line. This dilemma warrants some thought. I have adopted the attitude that if I am doing my job by getting out into the marketplace, my clients are going to know how to reach me.

Most phone companies across the country are making a real effort to service the booming home-based business industry. It is worthwhile to drop by your local phone store outlet to see what they have to offer. While you are there, don't forget to ask about various long-distance options.

E-mail

The war over the advantages and disadvantages of the Internet, web sites and e-mail seems to be never-ending. Let me try to put this in perspective by using an example. Think back ten years and try to recall how many businesses and homes had fax machines. The answer is darn few! Today if you happen to encounter a company without a fax number you might have serious reservations about that organization.

Soon e-mail will be as common as the fax is today. I am at the point now where I look at business cards to see if my associates are utilizing e-mail. The perception, right or wrong, is you are leading edge if you have e-mail. As a newly formed consulting firm, don't you want to be seen as leading edge?

Anyway, I'm selfish — I like e-mail for casual business communications because it reduces my long-distance costs.

SUNDRY OFFICE EQUIPMENT

Based on a very unsophisticated survey, I have concluded the vast majority of independent consultants are office supply store junkies. As a self-proclaimed office-gadget junkie myself, I offer a few choice items to consider for your shopping list. What the heck, you are in business for yourself, so you might as well enjoy a few of the perks your accountant can legitimately write off.

Paper Shredder

Not only does the paper shredder slice and dice confidential material, it also keeps you in the good graces of your family environmentalists.

Besides, I have a personal philosophy that shredding paper is therapeutic for stressed-out entrepreneurs.

Electric Staplers

Nonbelievers initially scoff at this seemingly useless toy. It is amazing to see how many quickly become converts when they assume secretarial duties and are faced with a hundred sets of material to staple.

Binding Machines

We will touch more on the subject of professional-looking presentation material in a future chapter. Most small consulting firms need a binding machine. Prices vary greatly, but the VPC Report Master is the best buy on the market if you do not need to bind more than forty or fifty pages.

Mini Cassette Recorders

If you find yourself doing a great deal of travelling, even in the city, a mini cassette is a fast and easy way to record your thoughts and ideas. Recording the essence of your discussions with existing customers or prospects can prove invaluable.

My comments in this chapter may seem a little lighthearted or flippant. Upon reflection they are, but one of the reasons for being in business for yourself is to enjoy what you do. For many of us, part of the enjoyment comes from being able to work where we want, while surrounding ourselves with the tools of our trade that make our daily toil more fun. Keep that line handy when your spouse next questions you about the real need for an updated piece of software or that electric three hole punch!

CHAPTER 6

Organization
Practical Planning — Image

In North America, companies spend tens of millions of dollars every year on maintaining, changing and improving their image. Image is everywhere. It can be as visual as a logo or it can be as intangible as how effectively a corporate giant has been able to instil service quality into employees.

Over the years, I have known a large number of consultants. The ones who have impressed me the most are those who have taken the time to develop and sustain their desired image.

By the way, the word is image, not facade. Some of the best known corporations think they have established an image, but what they have really created is an illusion — sometimes one that is fairly transparent to clients and customers. In your consulting business, the image you portray must reflect who you are and what your company stands for.

So what are some of the influencing factors you will wish to consider as you contemplate your image? What is that image based upon and how do you transmit it to existing and potential clients? In the next several pages we will look at some of the factors you should review as you begin to define the image you want for your consulting practice.

MY COMPANY NAME IS?

I suspect you have already chosen your company name, or at least you are toying with three or four possibilities. In some situations, having the right name is extremely important, and in others, it is not as high a priority. Let me offer some examples.

Reg Pirie Incorporated

This completely legitimate name tells you very little other than that Reg Pirie has a corporation.

Reg Pirie & Associates Inc.

By adding a couple of words, you get the sense that Reg Pirie is the lead person, likely the founder, of an incorporated company that has full-time or other associates.

Pirie Management Consultants Inc.

Another few changes have created a different impression. The name Pirie still denotes the involvement of a certain individual or family but the phrase "Management Consultants" indicates the nature of the business.

Ink Ink Publishing — A Division of Pirie Management Consultants Inc.

Ink Ink Publishing is a trade name. "A Division of..." conveys the idea the incorporated entity is more than one-dimensional. The use of trade names is something you should discuss with your lawyer. They can be an easy way of segregating different types of business under the umbrella of your limited company.

GAP Associates

This company name tells you very little. My wife and I used this name a number of years ago, and we learned several lessons the hard way. We thought it was neat. Why? Because we ran a business dedicated to helping companies teach employees how to do better.

We thought the word gap could be used in a variety of innovative ways, such as "Bridging the Learning GAP" or "Discover the GAP Between Perception and Reality" and so forth. Unfortunately, "What do you do?" was the most often asked question from confused potential clients.

At the end of the day, there are no hard and fast rules about selecting a company name. Including your name (first, last or both) does transmit the important fact that the company is personally run. Add-ons such as "partners" or "associates" sends a message that you are bigger than a single-person operation or you have a cadre of professionals you can call upon.

If you follow your company name with an illustrative phrase, readers will be less inclined to be baffled about what you do. Going back to GAP Associates: we could have solved many problems by inserting the phrase, "Consultants in Employee Excellence." The add-on could have also appeared on the letterhead and business cards.

If you choose to go with a descriptive name, give careful consideration as to whether it will stand the test of time. Hi-Fi Engineering Ltd. is not going to convey much of a message today unless you are over the age of forty. In retrospect, Beta Audio Video Consultants Inc. might have been an equally poor choice.

Similarly, you do not want to restrict yourself in your description. Grant & Jones Benefit Consultants Ltd. might wish they had originally gone with Grant & Jones Compensation Consultants Ltd. when they eventually decided to expand the scope of their business.

Have your lawyer check to make certain your company name has not already been registered in your province or federally.

LETTERHEAD AND BUSINESS CARDS

If you have one or two creative bones in your body, designing a letterhead and a business card can be fun. In the event you are totally lacking in creativity, it can be exasperating. In either case you will want to review some of the words you jotted down earlier to describe yourself and your company. Think about the different visual images conjured up by the descriptive words "conservative" and "hi-tech" for example.

The letterheads and business cards for a conservative company would differ considerably from those used by a hi-tech company. The word *conservative* immediately causes most of us to think about colours like black, navy or maroon. The lettering might be Times Roman and the layout would be traditional. Think of a letterhead used by a long established legal firm.

The hi-tech company would have a different look. Ink selection would be dramatic and colourful. There might be two colours, lettering might be modern and layout could be more stylized.

I am not suggesting there is a right or wrong approach when it comes to choosing a style. Be conscious of what image you want to convey. You might also want to do a little research to see what your competitors are doing.

Take the time to look at some business cards and letters you have in your files. See if something catches your eye that might be appropriate for your company. You might also want to crank up your computer to see if one of your programs has sample letterheads and business cards. (I would not encourage you to use one of these without making modifications. You do want to portray a degree of originality.)

Should you be tempted to go with a logo, proceed with caution. An originally designed logo can add a distinctive touch to all your material. On the other hand, using one that comes out of a printer's stock logo catalogue can have less than satisfactory results. In my early working days in Calgary, every consultant in the oil patch seemed to have the same oil derrick logo somewhere on their letterhead. Not exactly the best way to set yourself apart from your competition.

Once you have a reasonably good idea of what you want, head off to see your printer. If you can do a working mock-up on your computer, this will be helpful to the printer. Don't be surprised if you are told that you will require camera ready copy. This means preparing the layout for printing. Some printers can do this for you, or they will direct you to someone who can.

Here are a few additional hints concerning printed material:

- Select good or excellent quality paper.
- Don't get carried away with fancy coloured paper. Remember coloured paper does not fax or photocopy easily.
- Consider the merits of recycled stock.
- When selecting paper for your letterhead, purchase the same stock for second pages and proposal material.
- Novice consultants often underestimate how much letterhead is needed. The cost of printing 2,000 copies is very similar to the cost of 1,000.
- It is less expensive to have all your printing done at one time, particularly if you are using non-standard ink colours.
- Your envelopes are part of your image and they should be co-ordinated with your letterhead and other material.
- If you need to use non-letter-sized envelopes, it is often more practical to have your printer prepare co-ordinated return address labels rather than printing the envelopes
- Business cards need to complement your letterhead. Don't use flimsy stock.
- Use the name you want to be called on your business card. Don't confuse people by using your full name if you go by a shortened version.

- Have all your phone, fax and e-mail information ready before you go to print.
- If you have affiliates in other parts of the country, you might want to incorporate those locations on your letterhead to illustrate you are not just a local firm.
- If you want to use your letterhead as the front page for bound proposals, make certain your left margin is wide enough.

A good printer will be an immense help as you develop your material. Printers can also put you in contact with a free-lance graphic designer, who will be equipped to translate your vague notions and concepts into reality.

Whatever you do, spend some quality time on developing the right visual image for your company. You want something that will send the proper message from day one, and with any luck, you will not have to make major alterations during the first three years of operation.

PROMOTIONAL MATERIAL

Somewhere in the first few chapters of this book I mentioned the need to have your initial promotional material ready before someone asks you for a copy of your business brochure.

While being prepared is important, I have found that most of us need some time to develop a final version of our information package. What you design for initial usage will vary greatly depending upon your chosen field. Some consulting practices need to go into considerable detail and others can begin with relatively simple formats.

One popular item is the folded brochure — one sheet of paper with two folds, giving you six columns. Such a brochure can be used to accent the highlights of your firm and can be followed up with a detailed information package. There are some pros and cons to using the format.

Disadvantages

- The two-fold brochure might imply you are small, not unique and unable to afford customized material.

Advantages

- The two-fold brochure is an inexpensive means of getting concise information to clients and prospects.
- The brochure can be mailed in a standard letter envelope.
- The prices are attractive and using a stock item avoids the need to design something yourself.
- You can print the brochures yourself, on an as needed basis.
- Changes to the content can be made with relative ease.

Unless cost is an absolute driving force, I would avoid using pre-printed stock formats when it comes to the two-fold brochures. But use the general format if it suits your requirements. Discuss the idea with your printer or graphic design person. You might be surprised how easily you can develop your own pamphlet, which is unique and co-ordinates with your own custom stationery.

You have two other options. You could design and print a formal brochure. This is costly. Or you could develop a comprehensive information booklet using desktop publishing software.

By going the latter route you retain the flexibility to make alterations and additions, particularly while your company is in the formative stages. In time you could convert to a more formal format. To add the all-important personal touch to the material you will be sending out, the first page of your brochure can include the name of your prospective corporate client, as well as the name of the individual contact to whom you are sending the material. This first page is often referred to as a fly sheet and can be printed to follow the theme or look of your letterhead. All that remains is to package the personalized fly sheet with your desktop-published insert into a jacket for binding.

What are the main components of the written material? Again, it can be very helpful to collect and digest what your competitors are using. No, the intention is not to mimic your competitors, but by reviewing their material you not only learn more about them, but you also get a sense of what you like and dislike.

As an example, you might look at three sets of material prepared by your competitors and find they are all the same. To set your company apart from the tried and true, you might want to make some significant alterations to format and content. Another approach is to ask some close business associates for input on what would be useful information for inclusion in a brochure.

Regardless of format and degree of detail, you are going to want to cover some basic items:

- what you do
- areas of specialization
- methodology
- qualifications
- what makes you different
- who does the work
- pricing
- references
- personal biography
- background of others
- mission statement / values / philosophy
- geographic coverage
- size and type of assignments handled
- how to connect with you
- web site address

If I were starting from scratch to prepare a corporate brochure I might begin with a few broad headings to help organize the information. The following paragraphs might get your creative juices flowing.

Where to Reach Us...

This is rather straightforward data but you do want to incorporate all this detailed information in a logical and presentable format. Don't forget the cell phone number, e-mail address, pager number and web site address. If accessibility is a virtue you want to emphasize, recording all of the above is important. It will send a strong message that you are serious about being reachable.

An Overview of XYZ Consulting Industry...

This is not necessarily an integral part of a corporate brochure. However, if you are in a consulting industry that has been experiencing significant change, this type of summary affords you certain opportunities to illustrate a number of points. You can accurately depict some of the historical issues that have affected your type of consulting. You can make a comment on what is happening at the present time. This can be followed by your opinion of what you envision taking place in the future.

Properly done, such a commentary will relay that you are knowledgeable and in tune with the future of your chosen field of endeavour.

What Our Corporate Clients Want to Accomplish...

In essence, the information contained in this particular section of a corporate brochure is a generic list of the results a client would want to achieve by securing your services. Obviously you can't get too specific, but if you carefully craft this material, your prospective clients will start to sense that what they want is indeed what your company has to offer. Later in this book we look at desired results in the chapter on proposals for service. You might want to scan the sample in that chapter to get some ideas for your corporate brochure.

Our Commitment to Our Corporate Clients...

Under this heading you can offer your prospects a clearer understanding of what you are all about and how you operate. This section could include: areas of specialization, methodology, differentiating factors, qualifications, geographic boundaries, your mission statement and some indication of exactly who performs the work.

Granted, you could record this information in a number of other ways but by tying it into your commitment to clients, you are sending a positive message about your company's values.

As an aside, there is an old advertising trick based on the fact you want to have readers nodding their heads up and down (not sideways) as they peruse your written material. The above four sections are intended to do just that.

Our Range of Consulting Services...

Here is where you zero in on precisely what you offer. Concentrate on the core services so as not to overpower clients with a long list. You likely do not want to be seen as a jack-of-all-trades and a master of none. If you are capable of handling other types of work beyond your core services, make an appropriate notation without being overly expansive. Accentuate the services where you excel.

Biographies...

This may be a very short section if you are the one and only consultant. A biography is intended to offer a snapshot of your professional background. Obviously, the content should confirm that you are qualified to provide the consulting services your company offers.The biography section also allows you to refer to others in your company or to individuals who supply adjunct support on a regular basis.

What Others Say About Us...

You may simply want to head this section References, but if you have been able to gather some endorsements, you might want to consider inserting quotes from those sources. A few suggestions:

- Always get clearance before using someone as a reference.
- Record where they work and a current phone number.
- Be satisfied that your reference is well regarded.
- Annually reconfirm the person is still willing to be a reference.

Professional Fee Schedule...

This section of your corporate brochure could range from one line to an entire page, complete with specific prices for each and every service you offer. The one line could simply say that each project is priced on an individual basis and you would be pleased to provide a quote.

If your type of consulting practice tends to quote prices, make certain you date the material to avoid any confusion if you change your fee structure. It is also a good idea to give yourself a bit of an out by using an expression like "Standard Professional Fee Structure". This gives you the latitude to alter the prices depending on the circumstances.

Preparing your promotional material can be a time-consuming labour of love, or it can be infuriating. If you become aggravated, you might consider farming out this undertaking. However, before heading off to see someone who specializes in such creative endeavours make certain you have a good handle on what you want to incorporate into the final version.

Professional writers or those skilled at desktop publishing can craft words and format the content, but they cannot put a heart and soul into your corporate brochure without quality input from you.

Remember, the material you send to clients will affect positively or negatively — the image you wish to portray.

ADVERTISING

The value of hard core advertising varies greatly from one type of consulting practice to another. I should clarify, when I use the expression "hard core", I mean the consistent use of print advertisements, TV commercials and radio spots.

Generally, not too many small independent consulting businesses spend inordinate amounts on such advertising. Perhaps the best method to determine if paid advertising is a route to consider for your company is to check out your leading competitors. Select three or four well-established firms in your field and track what they do in the way of advertising. It is fair to assume they would not be spending money over a long period of time if there weren't some reasonable payback.

The next level of advertising involvement might best be described as one-shot ads. These are usually printed material. A few examples warrant consideration, depending on your budget:

- advertising in a professional journal closely tied to your field of endeavour
- a newspaper ad specifically linked to a feature article or section in your local paper
- a small ad in a professional directory
- print advertising associated with a specific upcoming convention or trade show
- advertising in your local Yellow Pages

Lastly, there are donation ads, which include your advertising participation in printed programs for good causes — the Scouts, your church, civic events, service club flyers and the like.

Can you quantify the results of advertising? Not likely, unless you get in the habit of specifically asking first-time clients where they heard about your services. Frankly, posing that question is a good habit to cultivate.

An ad person once told me that small service-oriented companies are more apt to utilize advertising if their target market is directly focused on individual buyers. Conversely, consulting firms that typically do work for larger organizations are much less likely to advertise. In the long run, most consulting businesses rely far more heavily on networking to attract new business.

CHAPTER 7

Organization and Research
·Small Details — Big Image Impact

The previous chapter concentrated on the common elements we associate with a company image. But your total image is often influenced by many less noticeable elements.

In an effort to start you thinking about those factors, let me toss out some small details that have a big effect on your overall image — both from a corporate and a personal standpoint. Some of these details may seem minor viewed in isolation, but remember, the fabric of your company is woven strand by strand. A number of seemingly insignificant items slowly come together to create the overall image you wish to put forward.

WHO ARE MY COMPETITORS?

I do not want to flog this issue to death, but it is crucial to understand what you are up against in the marketplace, and that means knowing the strengths and weaknesses of your competition.

My cardinal rule is never to dump on a competitor, and at times I even praise certain facets of their operations. By taking the high road, you are demonstrating that you are well informed about what is going on in your industry. Similarly, by being gracious about your competitors' abilities, you are exuding a confident air.

HOURS OF BUSINESS

While your formal hours of business are a personal preference, they are driven in part by competition and client demands. If accessibility during non-standard hours is a key issue for your clients, you may want to play up the fact that you are consistently reachable beyond nine to five. This can be achieved by using your cell phone as a direct line number.

I have always used personal accessibility as a differentiating factor in my consulting businesses, and I have never found corporate clients abuse my offer to call me anytime. When they do call during off hours and I respond, that extra degree of customer service is embossed forever on their minds.

TELEPHONE ANSWERING

If you are truly an independent consultant, chances are your clients are not going to reach you personally every time they call. In this technologically driven era, voice mail messaging is a generally accepted fact of life. The vast majority of clients will not be in a huff if they are asked to leave a message. But it is important for you to establish the reputation as a consultant who returns calls in a timely fashion. If your recorded message says to callers that you will be back to them within three hours, you have made a commitment to do just that.

What about your recorded message? You will receive lots of unsolicited advice on this subject. Some will suggest you should have another person record the greeting message so it sounds like you have a secretary or an assistant. Whether you do or don't have such support in your office, I still opt for a personal message as I find the other route to be somewhat ostentatious.

Don't just record any old message, complete with hesitations, stammering and printer noise in the background. Jot down precisely what you want to say and practice it a few times. You not only want to get the words right — you also want to convey the right tone. I don't know about you, but I am seldom impressed by a monotone message when I reach a recording. Be up, be friendly, be genuine, be yourself, and keep the message to the point. And be certain you can meet your stated commitments relative to providing a timely reply. Here are two samples:

"Hi, this is Reg Pirie speaking and you have reached my voice mail. I'm sorry I have missed your call but please leave me a detailed message and I'll get back to you within three hours. Thank you for calling."

"Hi, this is Ink Ink Publishing and you have reached Reg Pirie's voice mail. I'm sorry I have missed your call but please leave me a detailed message and I'll get back to you prior to 5 o'clock today. Thank you for calling."

It might be worthwhile to employ an answering service. If you do, check their references. An answering service that is dependable, friendly and helpful only 90% of the time is not good enough for your company image. Once you find a high quality answering service, establish exactly what you want done and keep the instructions straightforward and consistent. Don't put the onus on them to determine what calls are important and which ones can wait. It is better to have them page you with every message.

If you are working from a home office, it is always preferable to clarify some ground rules for the family. You don't want five-year-old Billy explaining to your biggest client that you are in the bathroom or having a snooze. A few commonsense rules are also needed in terms of interrupting Mother or Father in the home office during normal business hours.

VEHICLES

I tend to be picky about some things — including how I maintain my vehicles. If you have clients in your car, your image can be on the line! A clean car, inside and out, sends a message to your passenger.

If you are not naturally fastidious about the appearance of your car, pay to have it washed and vacuumed on a regular basis. I will always recall being picked up by a consultant who was taking me to lunch. His car, while relatively new, came complete with an overflowing ashtray, enough dust on the dashboard to record a phone number in and sufficient clutter in the back seat to hide the family dog and maybe one small child. Somehow this disaster scene always leapt to mind when he would call to ask why I was not directing any training assignments to him.

Speaking of cars, you might want to consider business type vanity plates. Frivolous? Yes, but I am always amazed at the number of people who come up to me and ask me what my INKINK plates stand for. Here are a few of my other favourites: CA4YOU, LANMAN, CPU4U, HRPRO, TAXPRO, AIRFR8, NET2U, CME4PR and PRXPRT. If you are so inclined, you can have a little fun advertising your business with vanity plates but admittedly, it is not for everyone — CUL8R!

PERSONAL PRESENTATION

Perhaps I am overly sensitive to the whole issue of personal presentation because of all my years in the re-employment counselling business. But there is merit to repeating the old expression, "Dress for success and be successful."

These days life is a tad more complicated due to the advent of business casual attire and the like. However, I firmly believe you need to know your clients and dress accordingly. I would much rather be faced with frequent compliments about my natty ties or highly polished shoes than comments to the contrary after I have left someone's office.

To my mind, the same theory applies to using a superior looking briefcase or portfolio and a high quality pen. Your image is an accumulation of small details. To set yourself apart from the competition, you have to strive to be the best, not just an equal.

BUSINESS CARDS

I periodically run into what I call business card hoarders. I once knew someone who had designed a great looking card, but he was almost paranoid about giving it out because it was so expensive. Business cards are for handing out! I guess the lesson to be learned is that the production cost of your business cards shouldn't inhibit the intended use.

Frankly, I always take satisfaction in having to call my printer to order more cards — I feel like I have done a good job in getting my name out to another 1,000 potential users of my services.

Let me emphasize a couple of other points concerning business cards. The card should be co-ordinated with your letterhead and the design should be uncluttered. A business card is not an advertising billboard.

One final item. Always record the first name you normally use. By offering your business card you are attempting to effectively introduce yourself to others. Why would you wish to complicate matters by having cards printed with William or Patricia if you are known to everyone as Bill or Pat?

POSTAGE METERS

Using ordinary postage stamps may seem like the natural thing to do, but consider a couple of image factors.

Do big corporations use stamps? The answer to that question is obviously no. Might you be seen as something less than a professional business entity if you use ordinary postage stamps? The answer is likely evenly split between yes and no. If you agree with that hypothesis, why would you take a chance on being viewed as something less than what you wish to be?

Most new consulting businesses grossly underestimate postage expenses and the hassle factor associated with keeping a ready supply of postage on hand. Trust me, take a half hour and investigate leasing a postage meter. In the long run it will save you time and you will put forth a more businesslike image.

COURIER AND EXPRESS MAIL

In today's fast-paced world, everyone seems to want information and material yesterday. While normal mail will accommodate most deliveries, you will undoubtedly run into situations where you will require courier services. If possible, select your courier services before the first panic request from one of your clients.

You will need to establish an account with your courier of choice, and that usually means getting in touch with your friendly banker about a credit check. Do it now and avoid having to attend to these matters when you get busy. Depending upon your needs, you might also want to lay in a supply of Express Post or Priority Post pre-paid envelopes. Even when your clients don't ask for special delivery attention, using a quicker-than-normal routing system sends a positive message about your commitment to prompt service.

COPYRIGHT, TRADEMARKS AND PATENTS

I am by no means an expert on matters relating to patents and I will quickly defer to the professionals in this field. However, I do know you will want to protect your original work. Copyrighting is easy to do and it is not expensive. You need only look up *Copyrighting* in the government blue pages of your phone book to locate where to call for information and instructions.

In some cases, going through the process may not seem worthwhile or necessary, but there are definite advantages. Being able to legiti- mately record a copyright notation says to a reader of your docu- ments that you have produced original material. Again, the issue of image can come into play. Registration of copyrights, trademarks, patents and the like might also prove to be very important if you ever want to sell your business. These are all matters that warrant discussion with your lawyer.

PROFESSIONAL FEES

Finding professional fees under the heading of image may seem strange but I will clarify why in a moment.

Setting a rate for your services and products is one of the easier tasks if you have taken the time to research the norms in your industry. Granted, your pricing may be higher or lower, depending upon some of the subtle nuances that set you apart from your competitors. In the event your prices are higher or lower, be prepared to justify why.

Perhaps the more taxing quandaries relate to the issues of when you bill and do you split bill, which is staged invoicing based on progress to date. What to do when you encounter unique situations? These are the issues that can affect your image.

Many people would say invoicing is nothing more than a financial transaction. My inclination is to say it is more of an art than a science, and this is why I think it can affect your image.

Over the years I have developed, refined and learned some rules about dealing with clients. Many of those rules relate to invoicing. Some treat invoicing as the culminating activity associated with a contract or assignment. My approach is quite different. I view invoicing as yet another step in building and cementing my relationship with a client. Applying some good old-fashioned common sense to the invoicing process can lead to repeat business and will enhance your image. Let me offer some views for your consideration.

Invoice Timing

Finished the job, time to invoice! In theory that is a great principle, and heaven only knows your banker will endorse rapid invoicing.

Personally, I like to give things a little time to settle. It is much better to wait a couple of weeks to be certain your client is totally satisfied with your work.

Another factor to consider is that if you bill immediately all the time, you can develop a reputation of being a little too money hungry. Worst still, clients might get the impression you are encountering financial difficulties, and no one wants to deal with a consultant who may be financially unstable.

Reducing Your Invoice

After you spend some time in the consulting field you will find there are a few occasions when the value of the work you have completed is worth less than the agreed contracted price. That is not to say your work was in any way inferior, but that the assignment was simply not worth as much as you and your client originally estimated.

In these situations you can usually get away with billing the whole amount, but you may want to consider another approach. Go back to the client, explain your concerns and suggest what you believe would be more fair and equitable. Taking such action sends a strong message to your client concerning your ethics and professional integrity. I might add, going this route makes it much easier to renegotiate in subsequent situations where the agreed price may have been a little on the light side.

Credits and Reimbursements

No one likes to give money back. However, you will encounter situations where you have already received your cheque but for whatever reason a credit or a reimbursement seems to be warranted. These situations usually crop up more often when consultants are prepaid for their services.

Take the initiative. Take action. Make the offer to do what you think is right and proper. In my many years of dealing with large corporations, it always amazed me how surprised people were when I offered a credit or some type of refund.

If fairness, equity and building long-term business relationships are on your agenda, issuing a legitimate credit or refund without being asked to do so will drive home those principles to your clients with greater force than any other action you take.

Can you do me a small favour at a reduced price?

Oh, I used to hate those conversations, because it usually meant I was being asked to do a cut-rate job at a cut-rate price. The real dilemma here is that you could be setting a precedent, both in terms of dollars and quality of work.

I finally arrived at a solution, which may or may not work for you. If the question was posed by an existing client and the request was less than $500, I did it free on a one-time basis. Oddly enough, I was rarely asked for another special deal, and for the most part I was given other assignments. As one of my old partners observed, you are almost shaming clients into the next deal because they feel obligated. That could well be true. In any event, your image remains intact.

When it comes to professional fees and invoicing practices, you need to establish a flexible policy underscored by fairness and equity. In some cases you may feel you were slighted, but taking the high road is invariably the right course if you want to expand your working relationships.

There are innumerable factors that will affect your image. Presenting a better image than your competitors will win you assignments when you are equally matched in other areas. Your positive image can even edge out competitors who might be technically superior to your company.

Your personal and corporate image cannot be a facade or an illusion. Your image must be based on truth, substance and integrity. Never take image for granted, as your success will be directly linked to how you portray yourself and your company.

CHAPTER 8

Organization and Research
Marketing Preparations

Okay. You are focused, you have a good handle on what your company is all about, you are arriving at some conclusions concerning your office space/location and you are actively considering how to create and sustain the proper image for your company. Now what?

It is time to figure out how to start paying all those bills that are collecting on the corner of your new desk. A well-thought-out marketing plan will start you on the way, but before you leap ahead, get organized and conduct some basic research.

This chapter will assume you plan to limit the geographic boundaries of your business to your local area. (If you have larger boundaries, the basic concepts would be the same but you will be relying on research from farther afield.)

THE PROSPECT LIST

Before you frantically start scribing various company names, stand back and look at the macro picture. Select six broad market or industry segments where you think your company may acquire contracts. As an example, you might choose pharmaceuticals, government, financial services, retailers, manufacturing and hi-tech.

You may want to give yourself some wiggle room by raising a seventh category called "other."

Plug these seven categories into your computer and spend the next hour brainstorming with yourself. Without referring to any sources except your own memory, jot down the names of companies under the appropriate industry headings. Now is not the time to be making unfounded assumptions. This is the beginning of a prospect list, and you should not be making any premature judgements about whether companies might ultimately be interested in your services. There will be time in the future to prioritize your list of potential clients within each category, ranging from the hot prospects to those you will follow up later.

Even at this early stage you may see some trends emerging as you review the seven lists. A couple of the lists may record numerous names, which might be a reflection of your previous business affiliations. If your past life involved working in the pharmaceutical industry, it would be only natural for you to be better acquainted with those firms. Or your "other" category may include several names that are in the same industry family. Perhaps you need another heading.

One or two of the categories may have a meagre number of company names. Don't necessarily give up on retaining these categories as industry segments you want to tackle. You will need to do additional research to develop a more extensive prospect list for these groupings.

Put the list aside for the balance of the day and move on to some other pressing issues. But don't totally forget about the list! As a new self-employed person, you must learn to be constantly on the lookout for new prospects. Seasoned pros in business development have a radar-like device that triggers the thought process to add someone to their ever-expanding list of potential contacts. This acquired skill comes with time and experience. For the fun of it, peruse your list tomorrow morning and see how many more company names your memory will yield.

Next you will do some real research. Sources of information vary dramatically from business to business. Here are some suggestions.

LIBRARIES

Libraries do still exist. They have not all been transported into cyberspace. Drop by your local library and go to the business section. I have found libraries and the people who work in them to be extraordinarily helpful and accommodating. Explain what you are attempting to accomplish and they will point you toward several reference directories that list companies by industry.

Your first visit to the library may turn out to be a reconnaissance mission. By spending several hours reviewing what is available, you will gain a sense of where to find data. Don't forget to ask if the library has access to on-line sources. This might come in handy when you need to research a specific company or if you need to track down material from back issues of a newspaper.

MUNICIPALITIES / CHAMBER OF COMMERCE

When you think about your local municipality you may automatically focus on mundane departments like the licensing bureau, the tax assessment office or road maintenance. The department you want to find is the business development arm of the city administration. Normally these offices are staffed by people who are eager to promote their city, and they can be of immense assistance.

Explain you are doing market research preparatory to starting up your own business. I would be surprised if you don't walk out with some solid information, and at the very least you will be supplied with several suggestions and other research sources. While you are there, check to see if the municipality has any newsletters. Put your new company on the mailing list.

The Chamber of Commerce will be another worthwhile stop on your research tour. You might also want to pick up literature about joining the Chamber of Commerce — it's often a great source of networking opportunities.

NEWSPAPERS / PERIODICALS

For any of you who have read my previous books, I would be remiss if I did not comment on one of my favourite sources of information.

Yes, it is that inexpensive bundle of newsprint that can be delivered to your door every day. For an independent consultant, newspaper reading is a must — both local and national editions. If you are an occasional reader, become a consistent reader. If you are a regular reader, become a fanatical reader.

I say this for two reasons. The first relates to image. Everyone enjoys dealing with a well informed person. Second, the newspaper is a wealth of information about your clients, prospects and industries in general. For the next week, read your newspaper from start to finish. Before you scan a news item, ask yourself if the article could possibly lead to a business development opportunity for your company. You will be delighted at the number of times you find yourself clipping out an article for follow-up.

It is easy to get swamped with magazines and journals, but if you do not already subscribe to one or two of the leading periodicals in your field, best order now. You don't want to get caught off guard when a client asks what you thought about some must read item in the current issue of *the* magazine in your industry.

Most consultants will agree it is difficult to stay current when you are working on your own. You do need to carve out a certain amount of time to keep up to date. Treat this as a part of your commitment to ongoing self-enhancement.

THE INTERNET

This subject was touched upon when we discussed the importance of having an e-mail address. In terms of information gathering or business research, the effectiveness of the Internet varies from nil to mind-boggling. Your utilization of the Internet for research purposes will depend in large measure upon your area of specialization. The issue of having your own web site will be addressed in a later chapter.

It would be well worth your while to check out the web sites of any company you are researching as a potential client. I am not an avid surfer of the net. But for those of you who are unfamiliar with the information super highway, let me give you a real-life illustration.

Not that long ago I was preparing to speak with a potential client whose company was located in a small community outside a major city in the United States. In a matter of half an hour, I had viewed the company web site and pulled up the web site their community had developed, complete with a map of the industrial park where my client was located. It was amazing how much more congenial the initial discussion was because I was armed with current background information.

NETWORKING INFORMATION SHEET

There comes a point when we all need to move beyond making lists of potential clients. I am not suggesting you abandon your master list. Indeed, you will want to regularly keep adding to it.

However, you do need to make some hard decisions. Which companies are going to receive your initial attention? Look at each category and select four or five company names you want to include on your marketing hot list. Your initial marketing thrust will be focused on six or seven categories and four or five business within each category. You might think tackling twenty-five to thirty-five prospects at one time is not that ambitious. Trust me, it is if you are doing it properly. Start slowly until you have a good feel for the amount of work involved in this undertaking.

The next step is to determine if you have any personal contacts in those companies. Don't be concerned about where those contacts work within the company. Let me clarify by using a brief example. Under normal circumstances you might prefer to speak directly to the head of the Management Information Services Department. Obviously you could take the direct route and find this person's name and start from there.

That course of action is fine, and in many scenarios you will do just that. However, you will discover it is far easier to get an audience with your preferred contact if you have a little extra leverage provided by someone you already know within the organization. Say you know the Director of Finance at your targeted company. He or she should be your first contact. Your challenge, via networking, will be to orchestrate an introduction to the Director of MIS by soliciting the assistance of the Director of Finance.

This is where being extremely well-organized begins to pay huge dividends. On the last page of this chapter you will find a sample of a networking information sheet. Take this general format and design something workable for your situation. Run off one copy for each company on your hot list.

For every sheet, pencil in all the information you currently have available. I suspect you have a number of blanks staring you in the face! This is where the tedious part of your research begins. Get on that fancy new phone you bought the other day and start to fill in the blanks. Note: if you happen to reach one of your contacts, this is not the time to launch into a discussion about what you are doing. Simply say you are updating your records for your new business venture and you will be reconnecting in the very near future.

If you don't know anyone in a targeted company, make a phone call to gather the pertinent details about the person you eventually want to meet. A word of advice — get all the information during the first call. This will include:

Exact Name of Company and Division

You may know a company is ABC Pharma, but in the near future you will be corresponding with a representative of the firm. If you want to make the proper impression, you need the precise name of the company. Also confirm the name of the division.

Address, Postal Codes, Phone Number and Fax Numbers

Check the exact addresses and postal codes. Where possible, request your contact's direct line phone number and/or extension. If you are dealing with a very large corporation with more than one location, determine precisely where your contact is situated. The address you are given may be correct for mailing purposes, but your contact could easily have his or her office in another complex.

Try to get a fax number for your contact. (If necessary, this information can wait until your first face-to-face meeting, when you exchange business cards.)

Exact Name and Title

In the not too distant future you are going to be corresponding with this person — someone you may have never met. First impressions are extremely important. You want to have the name absolutely correct in your introductory letter. You know the reaction you have when your name is spelled incorrectly!

To complicate matters, the person answering the phone at ABC Pharma may tell you your contact's first name is Patricia. Watch those tricky first names. Does your contact go by Patricia or Pat? Ask for clarification. You want the proper salutation to appear on your introductory letter.

Here's a tip. If the person you are talking to does not know, phone the contact's direct line number. Chances are you will get a recorded voice mail message. Nine times out of ten the message will answer your question.

Let me expand on this seemingly minor point. If I receive a letter starting "Dear Reginald", I immediately think the sender found my name on some mailing list. Either that or my mother is upset with me. My inclination would be to ignore the correspondence, because the writer has not taken the time to get my name right. These little things can knock you out of the running before you even get around to explaining why a company should consider dealing with you. Pay attention to small details and you will set yourself apart from your competition.

Also, confirm your contact's correct title. Many people are sensitive about their titles. Don't rely on information that you presume is accurate. What would you think if you received a letter addressed to the Assistant Director of MIS, when in reality you had been promoted some six months ago to the Director level? Using the right title in your correspondence demonstrates your attention to detail, and at the same time it is just plain common courtesy.

Why have I gone into such detail about gathering this data? So you will learn to keep your life simple by being very organized. Once you have assembled the necessary information, plug it into your data base and you won't have to worry about it again until the information starts to change.

For now, you have everything at your fingertips to communicate with your chosen contacts. Assuming you have input all the data correctly, your client information software will do the work for you. If you want to be organized, efficient and successful, you must have and use some form of client information software.

By now, you have assembled a good portion of the material you will need to start developing a more formal marketing plan. In the next chapter we will distil much of what we have learned to this point into a draft marketing plan.

NETWORKING INFORMATION SHEET

NAME OF INITIAL CONTACT	
TITLE	PHONE #
COMPANY	
ADDRESS	
POSTAL CODE	
GENERAL PHONE #	FAX

OTHER CONTACTS SUGGESTED BY INITIAL CONTACT			
NAME	PHONE	TITLE	COMPANY/DIVISION
1.			
2.			
3.			
4.			

NOTES

CHAPTER 9

Organization and Research
Marketing Plans

Some will argue that preparing an actual marketing plan is not necessary. I strongly disagree for the following reasons:

- A Marketing Plan does not need to be an unwieldy document but it can help you focus on what you intend to accomplish during the next twelve months.

- Laying out pre-determined goals in a Marketing Plan will allow you to measure your progress and activity.

- Setting forth achievable deadlines will aid you considerably when pacing yourself in your business development activities.

- Recording realistic yet challenging targets will allow you to motivate yourself as you implement each phase of the plan.

- A Marketing Plan will give your friendly banker a much better sense about how you intend to logically build and expand your new business.

What exactly is a marketing plan? It plots the activities associated with acquiring new business and maintaining existing connections. The plan is anchored on some very basic assumptions about your company:

- core products and/or services

- guiding basic values
- service delivery methods
- differentiating factors
- targeted clients

When you write your marketing plan, you will be outlining your general philosophies concerning marketing. You will also be delineating the marketing interventions you plan to make in the upcoming twelve months.

While it is important for you to have a plan, it is equally crucial for you to build in flexibility. Why? Because your plan must work around the assignments you undertake. For now, you do not have the luxury of a dedicated marketing person!

One of the biggest challenges of an independent consultant is to maintain and sustain a marketing presence while at the same time completing the work he or she is being paid to do. If you don't have a flexible marketing program you will be faced with a feast-or-famine livelihood. The trick is to avoid the peaks and valleys.

In short, you want to be earning money consistently and constantly. At the same time you want to press forward with the marketing initiatives that are critical to keeping those new assignments rolling in regularly. It is a vicious circle. Not being able to maintain the proper balance between revenue generation and marketing has been the downfall of many a good consultant. Crafting and following your plan can make the difference between not making a living and being very successful.

Now we'll look at how to plan a flexible approach to marketing.

PERSISTENCE IN MARKETING

Not everyone is going to want to immediately purchase your services. They may have existing suppliers who are filling their needs, or they may not require your services at this point. Indeed, potential buyers may legitimately believe they will never use your services.

Your challenge, through an ongoing and long-term marketing program, is to positively position yourself so that when a need arises, you are one of the suppliers called upon to put forth a proposal for service. The unsuccessful consultant is one who makes a couple of contacts or marketing interventions and when rebuffed drops the client as a prospect.

Let me offer a story about one of my potential corporate clients when I was in the re-employment counselling business. After going through my usual tenacious efforts to get an audience with a decision maker, I found the company never used career transition services. This was not a put-off — it was a statement of fact.

Now, I could have written that firm off as a complete and utter waste of time. But my marketing philosophy is predicated upon being uppermost in the minds of potential clients when circumstances change. To do this effectively, you must maintain a persistent yet professional presence. Some two years later, this corporation experienced a major shift in direction, which created a need for re-employment counselling services.

My ongoing marketing efforts resulted in business some twenty-four months after the initial rebuff. Marketing and business development are long-term investments in relationship building, which can pay off handsomely if you have the patience and persistence to keep yourself in front of a corporate client.

Having spent two years maintaining timely contact with my decision maker, I jokingly asked him why we were given the business when their policies changed. The answer: my contact felt he had come to know me, he enjoyed the material I had shared with him, I had not been a pest and he admired a person who was persistent.

The above may be the most important lesson any of us can learn about the beneficial results of developing and implementing a logical, long-term marketing strategy. Perhaps Calvin Coolidge summarized it best:

"Nothing in the world can take the place of persistence. Talent will not; nothing is more common than unsuccessful men with talent. Genius will not; unrewarded genius is almost a proverb. Education will not; the world is full of educated derelicts. Persistence and determination alone are omnipotent."

With those thoughts in mind, let's look at what your marketing plan should include. This is not a pro forma marketing plan. Pro formas are for people who want the quick and easy way to complete a task without having to put much personal thought and energy into the exercise.

This is a guide to stimulate your thoughts and aid you in the development of a comprehensive plan specifically designed to suit your needs. Expand it, contract it, change it, but above all else, spend quality time organizing how you and your company will be positioned to take advantage of future opportunities.

SCOPE OF SERVICES

Under this heading, include what you intend to sell — the bread and butter items that will comprise the core of your services.

Any secondary services should be listed separately. Should your long-term plans include expansion into other areas, record these and make note of when those services might become available. If you will need extra time to develop expanded services, note what you will need to translate those visions into reality.

PRINCIPLES, VALUES, GUARANTEES, METHODOLOGIES AND DIFFERENTIATING FACTORS

In this section outline your guiding business principles and your standard operating procedures or methodology. Face it, not many of us would state we were going to operate in a slipshod fashion and make money with no regard to the well-being of our clients. On the other hand, you don't want to make lofty claims that are untrue and unobtainable.

It is important to articulate those factors that underpin how you will conduct yourself and your company. In essence these are the words that define your image. Also include a clear statement concerning what differentiates you from the rest of the competitive pack. In many cases, those differentiating factors will significantly affect your methodology — how you go about delivering your services.

At the end of the day, you will also need to decide how you are going to guarantee or stand behind your work. You might also want to consider how your company proposes to track customer satisfaction.

GEOGRAPHIC BOUNDARIES

This subject has been broached on several occasions but it needs to be included in the Marketing Plan for sake of clarity. If nothing else, recording boundaries will discipline you to methodically concentrate on a predetermined area.

If you speak to consultants who have been in business for a number of years, they will likely concede that one of their early mistakes was not keeping focused on where they were doing business. Once you start to stray beyond your range, you run the risk of becoming inefficient.

There are obviously exceptions, but those situations should be assessed carefully before you make a commitment.

SERVICE PROVIDERS AND QUALIFICATIONS

Me and I'm great! The foregoing could be the abbreviated response to explain who will do the work and why you are qualified. Notwithstanding the truth of the statement, a somewhat expanded and better crafted commentary is warranted.

In all seriousness, emphasizing that you are the major service provider has merit. Record why you are qualified to deliver the services outlined in your marketing plan. If you have partners, associates or temporary adjuncts, explain who they are and why they are qualified to be part of your team. You might wish to append professional profiles for everyone, or a biography page may be sufficient.

Let me digress momentarily to make an observations about the emerging importance of consulting affiliations. Most consultants have a relatively narrow field of expertise. If you try to be all things to all people, you run the risk of overstepping the bounds of your competence. However, there are times when an assignment calls for expert input that is outside your scope.

Progressive consultants are problem solvers, but that is not to say you personally need to have all the answers. If you take the time to develop a mutual working relationship with other professionals in adjacent or related fields, you are able to legitimately advertise that your services provide linkage with an expanded team of qualified individuals.

I raise this point for your future consideration. In time, if you develop such affiliations, you will want to include this fact in the Service Provider portion of your marketing plan. This can be a very powerful and persuasive way to attract new business.

You can be seen as the problem solver who knows where to call for specialized services.

KEY AREAS OF MARKETING CONCENTRATION

You have made a list of which market or industry segments you expect to acquire business from. The list will be called Key Areas of Marketing Concentration. By recording this information you are crystalizing your marketing focus for the upcoming year. This is your first marketing plan, and will be the foundation for all your future marketing endeavours.

Your list will allow you to zero in on very specific target groups. Choose the primary companies that will receive your initial attention, and identify which companies you consider secondary prospects and alternate sources. By doing so you are prioritizing your hit list. In all likelihood, the list will not remain static and you should record how many other business sources will be added during the next twelve months.

MARKETING PHILOSOPHY

Your marketing philosophy is a very personal and subjective statement of your overall approach to marketing and to your clients. Some will suggest you should treat high potential clients differently than those considered to be lower on the scale. I am not convinced that assigning a rating system to clients is necessarily the right course of action.

Every prospect has the potential to become a good paying client. Reality dictates that some will have higher potential than others. Unless you are extraordinarily intuitive, you won't know who will buy your services and when, at least during your formative years as a consultant.

Let me give you an example that might influence how you decide to treat the people you meet in your daily business activities. After six months of meetings and discussions, I eventually landed a very modest contract via a lady who had been employed by her company for a number of years. Additional contracts were sporadic, and the dollar volumes were minimal.

Now I could have paid her less attention than I was giving to representatives in other corporations who were awarding me much more lucrative assignments. But that is not my marketing philosophy. She was kind enough to direct what business she had available to me, so she deserved to be treated as well as my other clients. Obviously I am referring here to relationship management time and not time spent on actual projects.

What happened? Eighteen months later she landed a new and much more senior position at a larger firm. As you might expect, when her new employer had need for my services, you know who was called upon to handle a very profitable assignment.

Marketing and networking are all about dealing with people, not just companies. In fact, when we get into the chapters about networking you will find the focus is definitely on people.

I cannot dictate what marketing philosophy you and your company should adopt. But I suggest you consider an approach that treats people with equal regard. The benefits are extraordinary if you are interested in building long-term and profitable relationships.

SPECIAL MARKETING ACTION PLANS, TIMETABLE AND CONTINGENCY PLANS

This is the nitty-gritty part of your plan. This is where you spell out precisely how you intend to reach out and establish contact with your business prospects. Your action plan will also record how you intend to work the account over time. Let me offer a sample of what I would include under this heading.

- During the first four months of operation, write to 50 known contacts at various companies to arrange a networking meeting, thereby establishing an initial rapport.

- In those situations where the contact is not a primary decision maker, arrange to network to the appropriate person.
- During months five and six, directly communicate with 30 additional decision makers in companies where you have no known contacts to secure introductory networking meetings.
- Follow initial written communications with three attempts to reach the targeted individual by phone.
- Even if you don't meet the contacts, send them your corporate brochure. In situations where no contact is made, a follow-up call will be made six weeks after the last attempt.
- Every contact will receive three additional written communications during the first twelve months of operation. Two of these three follow-up communications will include reference material such as:
  - a pertinent article, an update regarding your services or another appropriate piece of literature
- During the Christmas season, send appropriate greeting cards to every person on the data base, regardless of whether a face-to-face meeting has been made.

You want to have a clearly defined plan of attack that can be used as a template to show how and when you interact with prospective and existing clients. The goals you set for yourself may vary, but mediocre targets are not good enough.

If you were previously an employee in a corporate environment, you might recall that overused expression "stretch targets". Well, to be a success as an independent consultant you need to impose super stretch targets on yourself. Your special action plan will become your road map to a disciplined marketing and networking campaign.

IMAGE ENHANCEMENTS /
SOFT MARKETING SUPPORT

The above section lays out very specific marketing activities. Over and above these undertakings, you also need to consider and record other marketing related initiatives that will support your direct contacts with prospective clients.

Soft marketing supports will enhance the image of your company and heighten your presence in the marketplace. What you are attempting to do is to get your name in the system so more potential clients become aware of who you are and what you do, including your areas of specialization.

Image enhancement strategies require as much consideration as any other portion of your marketing plan. How you go about this will depend to some extent on your type of business and also on your personal comfort level relative to the extracurricular activities. Here are but a few examples:

Service Clubs

Becoming a member in a service club is not something everyone enjoys. Such clubs do give you a great opportunity to meet other businesspeople, and few of us would argue the merits of the community work accomplished by these organizations.

The decision to go this route is obviously a very personal matter. A cautionary note for the newly self-employed: don't overextend yourself by taking on too many club responsibilities in the first year. There will be time enough to increase your participation once you have your company on firmer ground.

Chamber of Commerce / Board of Trade

The advantages of joining either of these two organizations parallel what you can accomplish by becoming involved in a service club.

The Chamber of Commerce and the Board of Trade focus specifically on business issues and networking. There is a great opportunity to acquire germane information from the guest speakers who tend to frequent their functions

Before leaping into a decision, check with some of your business associates and maybe attend a few meetings to see if this is a good fit for you and your company. The cautionary note I raised under the service club heading also applies to this area.

Professional Associations

Joining a professional association can be an excellent way to meet a wide variety of other businesspeople who might utilize the services of your company. At the same time, such associations can provide a great venue for you to keep current on what is transpiring in your field of endeavour.

Sponsorships

This is a more overt method of getting your name in front of the public. It is certainly not a route chosen by every consultant. One of my associates is involved in minor hockey, and sponsoring a team is his way to give something back to the community while at the same time putting in a good word for his company.

I know people who annually sponsor a hospitality suite during the yearly conference put on by their professional association. The list of examples is endless. You do need to bear in mind the cost, even more so while you are starting up your company.

Community Work / Charitable Organizations

If the service club route is not something you want to consider, perhaps you can think about volunteering your time to a charitable organization or some other form of community work. This is an excellent way help out, while at the same time meeting a wide variety of people.

Guest Speaking and TV Appearances

By becoming a consultant, you are saying you are an expert in a certain area. Take every opportunity to get your message across to various groups. Often you are not selling your services or products, but you are using a speaking venue as a means to illustrate your knowledge about topics relating to your business.

If you systematically make yourself available as a guest speaker, you will be amazed at how quickly people begin to naturally think of you as *the* expert. Public speaking can also lead to TV or radio appearances on business shows or as a panel member at a symposium. Speaking is not for everyone, but remember: it's important to make effective presentations.

Articles in Newspapers, Magazines and Journals

Getting your name in print is a good way to build awareness about your company. Not everyone is a professional writer but stop and consider just how many times you have been asked to prepared a formal written document.

Before you put pen to paper or fingers to the keyboard, take the time to review some of the newspaper or magazine articles written by your peers. You might discover that the observations you have put forth in a recent proposal for service are easily transformed into an interesting and informative article.

Nothing ventured, nothing gained. Do a little rewriting and editing and send your article to a couple of potential users and see what happens. You might want to start off small by offering your work to an organization that has a newsletter relating to your type of business. If you know someone in the publishing business, phone and get some input.

Book writing might be quite another matter, only because of the amount of time required. But who is to say that you can't get started now and complete your first effort over a period of time? I can tell you that having a published book to your credit is good for your image.

Conventions / Trade Shows

There are multiple benefits to attending conventions and trade shows. First you get a break from work. Second you have an excellent opportunity to rub shoulders with others in your industry, including potential clients. Last but not least, you will have a chance to get caught up on some of the innovations in your field.

If you become involved in all these activities you could well find yourself lacking any personal or family life. Or you can become so engrossed in these activities that they begin to encroach on building your business. You need to achieve a good balance.

When you write your marketing plan, select two or three new projects that will enhance your image. Don't forget, being in business for yourself should be fun. Your undertakings should not only satisfy business needs — they should also afford you an opportunity to participate in something you enjoy.

Make the commitment to get started and set yourself deadlines for each undertaking. By getting involved in peripheral activities you will gradually begin to enhance your image and presence.

At the outset of this chapter I voiced my opinions concerning why each and every independent consultant should prepare a marketing plan. Many novice consultants avoid this seemingly unnecessary and time-consuming exercise because it appears to add limited value.

I acknowledge there can be a sense of urgency to get on with finding business, particularly after you have expended so much time and effort on planning other aspects of your business venture. But a well prepared marketing plan is a contract. It is a contract with yourself.

Being an independent consultant is often a lonely existence, and it is very easy to deviate from your original charted course. Varying from your intended path is just that much easier if you have not had the discipline to write down what you are going to do and how you are going to achieve your goals.

Don't take any shortcuts. Develop and record your flexible marketing plan and work toward the predetermined goals you have imposed upon yourself.

CHAPTER 10

Activity
Turning Plans into Actions — Networking

To this point, you have been preparing to begin the methodical task of introducing and marketing your new company to clients. A day of reckoning eventually arrives when you must turn all the planning into action and activity.

Throughout this book you will encounter one word over and over and over again. That word is *networking*. Many individuals can make a living as an independent consultant. But if you want to meet all your goals, you must learn how to be an effective networker. The ultimate successes will be achieved if you also learn how to truly enjoy networking.

Independent consulting businesses are primarily focused on selling services. In most cases you are actually selling yourself. Your potential buyers need to see you, meet you and understand what you have to offer. You cannot accomplish this by sitting in your office. Enter *networking*.

What is networking? The explanations and definitions of this sometimes mysterious phenomenon are long and varied, but when you get right down to it, networking is about people. You could go a step further and say networking is about people-relationship management. Companies, your potential clients, are run by people. You may be paid by companies, but people make the decisions. Think for a moment about all the decisions a potential contact person may make in terms of you and your consulting business. One person will decide if he or she:

- liked your introductory letter
- will answer your follow-up phone call
- will grant you an introductory meeting
- was impressed by you and what your company has to offer
- will review your corporate brochure
- wants to consider you for a test assignment
- will give you a chance to bid
- will support or select your proposal
- is pleased with your work
- will want to use your company for future projects
- enjoys working with you

These decisions and a host of others are all made by people. Some experts contend that networking is nothing more than a process to garner business. I would be inclined to say networking is not just a process — it is a state of mind. As a networking professional you must focus on people and opportunities. The entire concept of networking is predicated on four principles:

1. Gather useful information by meeting people.
2. Constantly expand your network of people.
3. Showcase yourself and your services to people.
4. Position yourself as a solution to decision making people.

There are logical steps to follow so your marketing efforts will be successful. Remember: maintain a clear focus, be well organized, attend to your research and sustain a high degree of activity.

In this chapter we will concentrate on the preliminary staging for the networking meeting and telephone follow-up. Subsequent chapters will deal with the actual meetings, the initial follow-up to those meetings and resultant proposals for service.

Before getting too far ahead of ourselves, I would like to again clarify that this book was written for those of you who are starting up your first consulting business from scratch. Having been this route myself, I have attempted to methodically and meticulously lay out what you need to do in the initial phases of launching your business. As such, the thrust of the section on networking is meant to get you introduced to a number of your targeted prospects. Later we will also look at ways and means of maintaining your network via various marketing interventions.

PRELIMINARY STAGING OF NETWORKING MEETINGS

We'll start with letter writing. In a subsequent chapter there is a set of sample letters. With a little creativity on your part these can easily be adapted to almost every situation — right from setting up a networking meeting to thank-you letters that will position you to develop and solidify a sound working relationship with clients.

The written form of communication will invariably set you apart from your competitors. Some say letter writing is a dead or dying art form and unfortunately, those critics may be correct. That said, well-crafted correspondence will open doors for you, because quality letters are an exception rather than the norm.

Letters are important for another reason: most people are averse to making cold calls. Of all the independent consultants in the midst of launching a business, only a handful of skilled communicators can run an effective marketing campaign solely by phone and one-on-one conversations.

Telephone calls and face to face dialogue are a huge part of networking, but effective written communications will ease the door open for meetings. Good correspondence will allow you to demonstrate the factors that differentiate you and your company from the crowd.

Turn to chapter 14, letter examples #1 and #2. Once you have written your standard introductory letters, you will want to dispatch them prior to following up by phone to secure a networking meeting. Both examples are intended to be direct and to the point. More important, they set the stage for your subsequent call so your contact will know why you are attempting to get in touch.

The first example clearly gives you an edge because you refer to a mutual contact. A person seeing this letter can do one of two things. They can check you out by communicating with the referenced person, or they can mentally accept the importance and credibility of your request by virtue of the fact that they respect the judgement of the mutual associate you have mentioned.

The second letter is for a cold call. Like the first letter, it paves the way for a follow-up call. While this letter does not give you the added advantage of a reference, it places you in a positive light with the recipient. These letters provide:

- an introduction
- a very brief history
- an explanation of your request for information
- a specific follow-up plan
- an acknowledgement of your correspondent's busy schedule

Both introductory letters acknowledge that you have started a new business venture. This is not the time to be obtuse about this reality. Note: you are not requesting the meeting to sell your services. You want some information from the targeted contact to assist you in developing the right approach for your firm. If you have done your homework, you will find the information you receive from your correspondent will align with what you already have to offer.

Now for those of you who still think grabbing the phone and making calls to unknown networking prospects is the best course of action, stop and reflect on the merits of writing a letter first.

Letter writing is by no means a guarantee you will connect when you call or that you will ultimately secure a networking meeting. But, when you make your follow-up call, the chances of a positive response will be significantly enhanced by your preliminary correspondence. If you do not like making phone calls in the first place, you will be able to refer to your recent letter instead of leaping directly into a dialogue with a stranger.

One last word of advice prior to moving to the telephone call. The people you want to reach are extremely busy, and your letter has specifically stipulated when you intend to make contact. You cannot control the mail system, but most of us have a sense about delivery times. It is preferable to have your letter arrive on a Thursday or Friday. Your follow-up will be the next week. What usually will happen is the recipient will glance at the letter and automatically place it in the "Things to do on Monday" pile because that's when you say you'll call.

On Monday, the letter is apt to be given a second reading, which will be a little more thorough. The highly organized person will likely toss it into next Friday's diary, assuming you will call by then or not at all. Keep your networking organized. You do not want to blow a great opportunity because you were not organized enough to make the phone call within the specified times.

THE PHONE CALL

So, it is time to pick up the phone and make the first call! This is one aspect of self-employment you may not have envisioned as being such a high priority. But consultants spend a great deal of time on the phone, positioning themselves for future opportunities.

You have a stack of twelve letters in front of you that all say you are going to be in touch this week. Can you be the only person in the world who is so nervous about something as seemingly simple as making a dozen calls? The reality is that very few people relish making calls of this nature.

To make matters worse, today's telephone technology appears to place hurdles in front of you, distancing you from the person you want to reach. It was bad enough when you had to do battle with an overprotective secretary or, heaven forbid, the central switchboard. Now you are constantly confronted by voice mail.

Even in the late 1980s one did not encounter many companies with impersonal phone systems. But as organizations pressed toward fewer support personnel, the number of voice mail systems increased dramatically. Some estimate that more than two-thirds of today's business calls magically disappear into a machine. A machine that records when you called, what you had to say, the inflection and tone of your voice and your questions.

The person you call can save your words of wisdom and play them back as often as they want. Even worse, you can be deleted by the touch of a button. Effective communication is critical to your marketing efforts, so it is important to understand what you are up against and how you can turn the electronic monsters to your advantage.

One of my favourite lectures is called "Taming Today's Telephone Technology". I ask participants to list the most common roadblocks in getting through to someone by phone. Here are the top six answers, in random order:

- The person is never in.
- They never seem to return calls.
- The voice mail is always on.
- The secretary always answers and screens calls.

- There is no apparent alternative to the voice mail.
- I simply don't like making the calls!

The last item on the list was by far the number one roadblock. When you couple your dislike of phoning with not reaching your prospect, it is no wonder you begin to resent the phone and become totally exasperated with the whole marketing process.

Wrong reaction! You are letting the phone system derail your marketing campaign. Look at the options you have when voice mail kicks in.

1. Hang up.
2. Listen and hang up.
3. Listen and press zero for a real person.
4. Leave a message.

Try option 2 and see what you can learn before you choose options 3 or 4. Here are a few examples of what you can glean from a recorded message:

- In most cases, the voice mail will give you the pronunciation of the person's name.
- You will get a sense about what first name they prefer. Is it Bill or William, Pat or Patricia?
- Many people record new messages at least once a day. Such a message might suggest when the person you've called will likely return to the office.
- Based on the flow of the recorded message, you can usually determine if the person is a regular user or even a strong advocate of the voice mail system. If he or she is, you are being given a clear signal that the person is comfortable with conducting business via recorded messages. In some cases, you might set up a networking meeting without talking to a real person.

- The message might contain names and numbers of others close to the person you are calling. Record this data — you may want to reach the person's secretary or associates.
- Some voice mail users say where they are and when they will be back, or whether they will be picking up messages.

By taking the time to listen, you will learn a great deal more about your potential contact. You might want to listen to the message, hang up, gather your thoughts and then call back to leave a well-articulated, professional recording.

Voice mail may not grant you a meeting, but you can use it to effectively showcase yourself and your company by emphasizing the points in your initial letter.

Let's highlight what you want to say in a recorded message.

- who you are
- when you phoned
- why you called
- what information you want to impart
- what action you intend to take — if any
- what action you want taken by the recipient

Take the time to craft your message so it sounds like you, and test it on your mini-cassette recorder or by phoning your own voice mail. Keep the message to less than a minute. You do not want the recipient to reach for the delete button because you sound like you are going to ramble forever!

The practise will ensure that your recorded message is crisp and to the point. And you will be building up your confidence for those occasions when you immediately reach the person you are calling. Here's a sample:

Hi, Bill (Good Morning / Hello). This is Reg Pirie calling and it is Monday morning the twentieth. I am phoning to follow up on my letter of September fourteenth. You may recall, Alan Jones suggested I get in touch with you.

As I mentioned in my letter, I have recently established a new consulting practise and I would appreciate your professional observations on a few matters relating to...............

Bill, let me stress, I am simply interested in gathering some much needed information. I recognize your schedule is hectic but when your time permits, I'd appreciate you calling me back at...

(Optional) - If I am not in, please leave a message and I will return your call as soon as possible. (Optional) - I should add, I will not be available on Tuesday of this week.

Thank you for your time and I hope we will be able to connect in the very near future.

The phone is truly your lifeline when it comes to networking and marketing, and it's also a vehicle to enhance your image. Don't be afraid to use it.

TELEPHONE TRICKS

Over and above what we have already reviewed, let me leave you with a few other tricks of the trade you may find useful.

The Secretary

Yes, there are still secretaries in the business world, and they deserve the utmost respect. Go out of your way to develop a friendly and genuine rapport, because if you are flip or tactless with them, you will substantially diminish your chances of getting through to your contact.

When you leave a message to have your contact return your call, automatically offer some detail about why you are calling. Often a simple reference to your earlier correspondence will be sufficient. After two or three pleasant exchanges with the secretary you might garner an idea about the best time to catch your elusive contact.

The Internal Phone Trick

Many phone systems differentiate between outside incoming calls and internal incoming calls. If your contact appears to be evading you, try phoning a number one or two digits removed from that of your contact. A simple, "Oh, I'm sorry, I must have dialed the wrong number, would you mind transferring me to ..." could get you through.

Keeping Track

In the note section of your computer data base, keep track of when you called and whether you left a message with a person or on voice mail. A simple "6m" or "6vm" will indicate you phoned on the sixth and it will also note what type of message you left. This is important to gauge when you should follow up if your request for a return call goes unanswered. If you left an unusual message, jot down the essence of what you said, such as: "Bill, I wanted to let you know I returned your call from earlier today but I am going to be out of town until and eighth and I will give you a call when I return."

Good Times for Marketing Calls

Sorry, no pat answers to this question.

That said, you can experiment by trying early in the morning, over lunch or after normal business hours. Voice mail fanatics often turn the systems off in the early morning hours to accept internal calls from other early-rising work associates. Some may answer their own calls while support staff are away for lunch, and many answer after five o'clock.

"I'm in the middle of a meeting..."

If you finally reach your contact but receive this response, it is not the time to attempt an abridged version of your dialogue. Simply ask when it would be a good time to phone back. Maintain control of the calling process and then follow through exactly on time. Even if you fail to connect the second time, you have demonstrated you are well organized and the type of person who meets your commitments. That can be enough to cause the contact to return your next call promptly.

Recorded Message: "I'm out of town for the next week."

Don't hang up. Use this as an opportunity to demonstrate your professionalism by confirming you called and say you will phone back a couple of days after your contact returns to the office. By doing this, you are suggesting you know how hectic it can be after being out of the office for an extended period of time. A little genuine empathy can be a nice touch.

Making the Calls

Decide when you are going to make your calls, organize all your background material and *get started!* Make several calls in a row, and you will find yourself developing a steady cadence and your confidence will increase after each conversation and message.

Set yourself a realistic goal for the number of calls you want to make. By getting them out of the way quickly, you leave the line free for incoming calls. When you are finished, you can turn your attention to other details of your business.

Before you phone, have all your information readily available. When you connect, visualize the person on the other end of the line, be yourself and talk as though you were face to face.

If you receive a call when it is not convenient for you, politely thank the caller for returning your call but explain you are not able to speak at that moment and you will phone back in five minutes. Your caller will appreciate the courtesy of a return call when you are able to devote your full attention to the matters at hand.

Be Up!

Any highly successful salesperson will tell you that you must be up to make good sales calls, and that is exactly what you are doing — selling yourself and your company. It is a fine line between not being up and procrastinating. Using the "I'm not in the phoning mood" excuse cannot last for more than two days. After that you are procrastinating, and you should give yourself a shot of self-confidence by reviewing this chapter.

You might ease yourself into a good telephone day by starting with a call to an old colleague or friend, just to get the blood flowing. Never let a bad telephone day cause you to avoid meeting the commitments you made in an earlier letter or during a previous call.

Notes

Take rough notes while you are speaking with a contact and immediately transcribe them to a proper format in your computer data base. Even reject calls deserve write-ups, because you may need the information in the future. If you do not accomplish the desired results during your call, ensure you conclude your conversation on a positive and polite note. You might well orchestrate another opportunity to see this person, and at the very least, you always want to demonstrate your professionalism.

Some Do Nots

Avoid making calls from your car phone unless it is absolutely necessary. If you do, at least pull off the road and be prepared with your notes. Do not call a contact at home or in their car unless you are asked to. Even then, they may not be concentrating on what you have to say.

Working the telephone part of your marketing campaign can be aggravating but it can also be rewarding. As any veteran salesperson will tell you, never stop calling when you are on a roll. That old adage may be mostly myth, but you can feel a heightened level of confidence after a good phone conversation, and you will transmit that enthusiasm during your next call.

Networking phone calls are a challenge, but they are almost always the precursor to actual networking meetings where you can advance your business opportunities.

CHAPTER 11

Activity
The Networking Meeting

Well, isn't this great — all the phoning has paid off and I have my first networking meeting scheduled. But what do I do now?

You no sooner clear one hurdle when another appears on the horizon. For many new consultants, the challenges are onerous because the entire experience is foreign.

Networking or information-gathering meetings might seem like a challenge, particularly if you still harbour the urge to rush into the meeting and ask for an assignment. Don't! If you do, you have compromised what you have said in your setup letter and your initial phone conversation. Worse still, the answer to your question will be negative. If by some strange quirk there is an opportunity ideally suited for your company, your networking contact will let you know.

You are conducting research — you have never said anything to the contrary. Let's look at a few other things to remember.

- This meeting is a discussion between two professionals.
- You are gathering information and researching.
- You are asking for input from an expert.
- You are enquiring about other sources of information.

- You want to expand your network.
- You are looking for other contacts in the company.
- You are *not* asking for an assignment!
- You are putting forth the image of your company.

Networking and information-gathering meetings are part of a continuum, they are not one-shot efforts. That is why networking must become a state of mind and not simply a process.

The networking meeting is vital to developing a rapport with people who may influence your business. Meticulous care is required before, during and after the meeting. If you are careless, you run the risk of jeopardizing a good opportunity. Learning how to handle these meetings properly will establish a comfort level, and you will form good habits.

BEFORE THE MEETING

Once you have secured the meeting, review all the material you have at your disposal. If you feel you do not have sufficient background information about the company, do a little more research. A trip to the library will give you access to recent news items about the company. Other resource material from the library may offer insight into the company's history. You may also want to check the company's web site.

There is nothing more embarrassing than getting into a networking meeting and having your contact ask your opinion about a recently publicized news item concerning the company, only to find you have not been keeping pace with current business events. If you are in business for yourself, part of your daily research is a careful perusal of newspapers. You will find this becomes easier once you have a good handle on those companies that form part of your marketing hit list. This will help you to zero in on pertinent and required reading.

If your meeting was set up with the help of a referral, give that person a call. They are part of your network, and by keeping them apprised about your progress, you are re-enforcing the fact you are actively pursuing business leads. At the same time, you can ascertain if your reference has any additional information for your upcoming meeting.

Review your research material and jot down what you want to find out during the meeting. This will allow you to structure specific questions to raise during the conversation.

How do you develop questions for your networking meeting? The first rule is to start with broad general questions and then begin to focus on more specific queries. Unfortunately, the conversation can take many twists and turns because you cannot control the other person's responses. By preparing questions you will be in a better position to influence the direction of the discussion.

Remember, you have three major goals during this meeting. First, you want to gather information. Second, you want to make a favourable impression. Last but not least, you want to expand your network.

Double check one other detail before the day of the meeting. Companies have a bad habit of having more than one location. They may use one street address for their incoming mail, but your contact could be situated in another building. Check! I am embarrassed to admit I have made this error more than once.

You have two last-minute items to handle. One is a personal image check, and while most people become annoyed when this subject is broached, it is extremely important. The other is straightforward: leave yourself lots of time. Improper preparation or arriving one minute before the appointment are two of the easiest ways to jeopardize a good meeting.

Now you might think it would be natural to leap right from here into the actual meeting. Not so fast — you still have to contend with the reception desk or waiting area, and you can on occasion learn a great deal during your brief stay in the outer office.

Usually, your first contact with the company will be a receptionist. Properly handling yourself in this situation can afford you an opportunity to mentally prepare and set the tone for your visit. Introduce yourself and politely explain who you are, who you are there to see and the time of your appointment.

An upbeat and confident dialogue with the receptionist will set the stage for your introductory comments to your contact. Don't forget, your contact may casually question the receptionist for an impression of you.

Arrive early and allow yourself a few minutes to complete one last check of your notes and questions. Then take time to absorb your surroundings and gather some peripheral information. It is amazing what you can glean from a ten-minute wait in a reception area. Here are a few examples:

- What does the area tell you about the company's image? It can range from stark and functional to understated elegance or downright palatial.
- What about the employees moving through the area? Are they formal, informal, chatting, relaxed, intense, upbeat, or sombre? Do they generally seem to dress in formal business attire, are they more casual or are they laid back?
- What is displayed in the reception area? Are there products evident? Or are the walls covered with expensive-looking art?
- What are employees talking about and what can you gather from those snippets of conversations?

Your observations can significantly assist you in formulating a feel for the company.

THE MEETING

Eventually, someone is going to appear — in most cases it will be your contact who has come to greet you in the reception area. If you have never met the person before, let them take the lead in introductions. This exchange will give you a chance to clarify some nagging questions. Let's look at a typical dialogue where Bill Smith is the contact and Reg Pirie is the visiting consultant.

Bill: "Reg, I'm Bill Smith."

Note, he is Bill and not William, and he is inviting you to use his first name. Get the names straight now. This is going to become an ongoing relationship, and you want to avoid any confusion. These are informal days in the business world. I can't think of many situations where you would address a contact by something other than a first name.

Reg: "Good morning, Bill, it is a pleasure to meet you."

If Bill is late, have a response ready that will set him at ease and let you create a favourable impression. For example:

Bill: "Reg, I'm Bill Smith, sorry for keeping you so long."

Reg: "Good morning, Bill, it is a pleasure to meet you. No problem, I was just catching up on my reading." Or, "No problem, I was just admiring your offices."

The long walk down the hallway is not the place to start your formal conversation. Keep the chatter light.

Once you get to your contact's office, make an effort to drink in the surroundings. Unless you are meeting off site or in a boardroom, the contact's office can supply you with a wealth of information about the person. Don't forget, your network is based on people.

For those of you who are unobservant, let me give you a few tips on what you can learn when you walk into a stranger's office. Marketing is serious business, but you can have a little fun with this amateur detective work.

- Marital Status? Wedding ring, picture of spouse on credenza
- Children? Pictures or refrigerator art work
- Divorced or separated? No ring and just photos of kids only
- Athlete or sports enthusiast? Sporting memorabilia
- Education? Sheepskins or certificates
- Professional affiliations? Plaques and certificates
- Hobbies? Pictures or related paraphernalia
- Work habits? Cluttered desk or the clear vista
- Company tenure? Plaques or pins
- Company stature? Size of office, furniture, floor location
- Computer fanatic? Lived-in look around computer station
- General interests? Books, artwork
- Formal or informal? Dress, posture, office layout

Use these and other minuscule clues to instantaneously develop a sense of this person. File that information away to use during your immediate encounter and for future reference. If you respond appropriately to the clues you will significantly enhance the rapport-building process.

Usually there are two items to deal with before the formal part of the meeting begins. Number one, exchanging business cards. Number two, accepting or turning down the offer of a coffee or a liquid equivalent. If you are a klutz by nature, politely decline by saying you have just had one. However, be gracious and allow your contact the option of going to get a refreshment.

If you are at ease sipping a coffee and talking, take your host up on the offer. You are two businesspeople getting together for a discussion. This is not an inquisition.

The Meeting Dialogue

You are in control, and for the most part, it is your agenda. There is no better way to prepare you for a networking meeting than to supply you with a typical dialogue, complete with comments.

This dialogue is slanted toward the networking meetings you will have in the first three to six months after establishing your company. The content and your approach will begin to vary and become more direct as time progresses.

The Meeting Dialogue — Rapport

"Bill, first let me thank you for taking the time to see me. I know Alan Jones said your schedule was very hectic these days."

Small talk will occur throughout this segment, and you will want to state the name of your referral for emphasis.

"I think I had indicated when I phoned that I would only need about thirty minutes of your time, but I can certainly understand if you have had to alter your schedule since we spoke."

Wait for a signal. If none arises, assume thirty minutes is okay.

"I am in need of some information relating to my new business venture.

The Meeting Dialogue — Purpose

"I am looking for some input from you regarding your company and the _____ industry in general. Alan felt you would be a good person to speak with, given your heavy involvement in this sector. I do have some specific questions to ask but perhaps if I give you a bit of background information about me and an overview of my new venture, the reasons for my questions will be more clear."

Keep the background detail very short and state the focus of your company.

"Over the past fifteen years, I have worked for two companies and since 1993, my career has focused on ..."

"Recently I decided to establish my own consulting firm, which is dedicated to... At present I am conducting some research in six or seven industry sectors to confirm that our core services are properly aligned to corporate needs."

Wait to see if any clarification is required and ask if it is okay to take notes. Start with your broad, general questions and move towards more specific questions.

The Meeting Dialogue — Questions

"Bill, do you mind if I take a few notes?"

"To allow me to better understand the ____ industry, can you give me your opinions in terms of some of the major changes and challenges you envision taking place in Canada during the upcoming three years."
"What action plans will your organization take to respond to those changes?"

"From your vantage point, are your competitors likely to respond in a similar fashion or are there other avenues that might be considered?"

"Let me just get back to the issue of competitors. If you don't mind my asking, who do you see as your major competition?"

"As I mentioned at the outset, my business focus is on____ an you give me some insight on what trends or changes you see taking place in that sector?"

"And how will your company be handling the ____ function in the future?"

"Given what we have discussed, I would certainly welcome your thoughts regarding how I have positioned my company."

Throughout the conversation, offer your own expert opinions when and where appropriate. This is your opportunity to positively showcase your expertise, but it is not a venue to show off!

The Meeting Dialogue — Recap / Close

"Bill, you have given me a great deal of valuable information. Correct me if I am wrong. Based on what you have said, it would appear that..."

"I will certainly review your information with the other data I have gathered. At the moment I don't have any other questions, but is it okay if I give you a call, should I need any clarification?"

"There is one other item that would be helpful. Based on our discussions today, can you suggest anyone else, either in your organization or elsewhere, that you feel could assist me in gathering additional information?"

If the answer is yes, get the details. If the answer is no:

"Well, if someone does come to mind, I would appreciate hearing from you."

"Bill, I have taken up enough of your time. Your input has been greatly appreciated. I will definitely follow up with Mr./Ms. ____. By the way, would you mind if I mentioned your name when I make contact? I will keep you apprised of my progress. If it is not inconvenient, I will send you a copy of my corporate brochure, simply for your records. Again, thank you for your time."

Don't linger, and keep within the thirty minute time limit.

As you will appreciate, it is difficult to make these dialogues generic and you will want to give a considerable amount of thought to your own line of questioning.

This is likely a good place to stress why consultants need to network. I am often asked why it is not just as effective to send a well written letter and your corporate brochure, with a request to select your firm for future assignments.

The answer is quite simple. Company decision makers are not going to make a purchasing selection based upon a brochure — even if you come highly recommended. A face-to-face encounter gives them a chance to size you up while getting a better sense of what your company can offer. In short, networking allows you the opportunity to make the right impression.

AFTER THE MEETING

You have done your prep work and you have had a good meeting. Do not stop there! The post-meeting work is every bit as important as the first two stages. Your dedication to proper follow-up is another way to set yourself apart from competitors. The technical procedures are simple.

- Transcribe your notes to your data base
- Prepare follow-up letter (see chapter 14)
- Write action items in your diary
- Where applicable, communicate with your original contact
- Write new referrals
- Keep in touch with your contact

Whatever you do, do not rely on the rough notes you might have taken during your discussions. Those are highlights only, and you will want to capture the details. The sooner you sit down to mentally review the meeting the better. Take the time to evaluate the entire networking chain of events, from your preparation to the final handshake. Record all your observations. Assess what you did right and what you could improve upon.

You should draft your thank-you letter immediately, while the nuances of the conversation are still crystal clear in your mind. You want to extend a sincere thank-you for the meeting, your contact's time and the valuable information you received. To demonstrate your alertness to the commentary, you may want to highlight one or two specifics. Confirm that you are going to follow up on any suggested referrals. This will illustrate your genuine interest in advancing your networking efforts.

And finally, make certain you leave the door open for future interactions. The next challenge is to keep your name in front of the contact so he or she will remember you when the right business opportunity arises.

If you have made even a passing comment that could have been construed as a commitment on your part, make note of it in your diary and follow through. You want to take advantage of every opportunity to demonstrate your sincerity and professionalism.

If you were originally referred to this contact by another, follow through again. Depending on the circumstances, the follow-up could be as formal as a letter or as informal as a voice mail message saying the meeting went well and you received a great deal of valuable information.

Communicating with new referrals is a matter of adding to your data base and activating the networking steps all over again. Finally, map out and diarize how you intend to keep in touch with your contact. Remember, networking is not a one-shot effort. You need a plan to maintain the contact. This can be done by confirming a meeting with the referral they gave you, by sending your corporate brochure, by forwarding copies of articles or by following through on some other issues you may have discussed. The future marketing interventions you take may differ from client to client, but generally you should be following the action guidelines you have established in your marketing plan.

Even for the most skeptical or reticent person, networking can be fun if approached in the proper manner. You will have great meetings, good meetings and poor meetings. But through planning, preparation and practise, your networking skills will improve in a short period of time.

You will know when you have achieved a degree of proficiency in networking when you realize that this approach will allow you to capitalize on future opportunities. Perhaps the best proof comes when a total stranger phones to inquire about your services because someone from your network passed along your name.

CHAPTER 12

Activity
Turning Networking into a Proposal for Service

There is no formula that magically equates a certain number of networking meetings with successfully securing a request for a proposal for service. The influencing factors are many and varied. Your consulting speciality, the local economy, your competitors, your degree of proficiency in networking, all these will dictate when you achieve this goal.

There is also no such thing as a fill-in-the blanks proposal for service. Content, layout, degree of analysis, length and sophistication of research will depend on the company you wish to approach and on your own style. However, some basic elements need to be incorporated into every proposal for service. We will address each of these in detail.

For those of you who have come from national or international conglomerates, putting together your first proposal for service can be somewhat unnerving. The concept may not be foreign to you, but your ex-employer might have used a standard format. Staring at a blank piece of paper or monitor can be a perplexing experience. All of a sudden, you realize the true meaning of the word *entrepreneur.*

To make matters worse, there is a degree of risk involved in submitting a proposal for service. If you are simply relaying great ideas, the company can keep your thoughts and implement the actions on their own. With this in mind, you must weave you and your ideas together so your suggestions are directly linked to you and your company.

A proposal for service is not something that can be dashed off in an hour. It will need to be drafted, edited, expanded, researched and re-researched. Given the situation you intend to address, there may be a need for more than the basic components but as a starting point, let's look at each of the usual major items.

To offer a more realistic overview of the proposal for service, we will use an abbreviated hypothetical example throughout the balance of this chapter. XYZ Company is in the mortgage business and has issued a request for a proposal relating to a restructuring initiative they wish to undertake.

THE ACCOMPANYING LETTER

This correspondence has six functions. You want to:

- recap what has transpired to this point
- subtly overcome any potential objections
- explain what is contained in the proposal for service
- offer to meet to respond to any subsequent questions
- stress your interest in the assignment
- pave the way for follow-up with the company

Your accompanying letter might look something like this:

First let me thank you for taking the time to outline the current situation being faced by XYZ Company. We are extremely pleased to be afforded the opportunity to put forward a proposal for service to address the upcoming corporate restructuring.

To be candid, we are cognizant of the fact that our firm is not well known to your organization. However, I believe the attached proposal, supplemented by our previously supplied corporate brochure, will provide you with a sound understanding of our values and our commitment to the people we serve.

Granted, that alone is not enough upon which to base a decision that could affect the lives of your employees. As I mentioned, our business is built on service to our clients and as such, we rely heavily upon the endorsements of our existing clientele, particularly when we have not had the benefit of developing a lengthy rapport with a prospective client. I would encourage you to carefully assess our credentials by speaking with any of the individuals noted on the enclosed reference list.

In an effort to set the stage for this proposal, I have taken the liberty of recapping some assumptions I believe reflect XYZ's current situation, the desired results and special factors for consideration. Certainly if you need further information, I would be pleased to reconvene to clarify any outstanding issues.

Bruce, we would welcome the opportunity to support XYZ during this difficult transition by co-ordinating and implementing the entire project. Perhaps the most appropriate way to summarize our commitment to the task at hand is to record our mission statement:

We provide fully customized corporate restructuring services...

Again, thank you for asking us to put forward a proposal and as agreed, I will be in touch with you on Thursday.

The above letter is only a sample and your covering letter will vary greatly depending on a number of factors. You will notice the second and third paragraphs deal in a very straightforward fashion with the fact that your company may not be well known to XYZ.

This may seem bullish but the approach does respond honestly and openly to a common concern when a major client is dealing with new or relatively unknown consulting firms. Since the subject is apt to come up anyway, you might just as well earn a few points by being forthright.

SITUATIONAL SUMMARY

During your various meetings with your contact, you have been gathering and recording information about the potential client. That data will be supplemented by the other research you have been conducting.

This is a summary. It should be a concise recounting of pertinent historical factors, a synopsis of the direction the company is considering and a restating of that new goal. For example:

The XYZ Mortgage Company was incorporated in 1972 and it currently services both residential and commercial client requirements through a network of 50 locations in Canada, situated in all major cities and several smaller communities.

While the XYZ Mortgage Company was negatively affected by recession-related trends in the early 1990s, the last audit of the portfolio suggests it is of better than average quality and all deteriorating situations are well in hand.

The current dollar mix of mortgages is 60% commercial and 40% residential. Over the course of the next two years, the company wishes to realign the commercial / residential mix to a 50/50 ratio, while significantly streamlining the administrative function to reduce operating costs by 15% from those levels recorded last year.

The reader of a situational summary should be left with the sense that you have captured the essence of what is going on and what goals are envisioned for the future. It is not always necessary or possible to concern yourself with minute details because you are not likely to be privy to all that information.

THE DESIRED RESULTS

In this section, state what the company wants to accomplish. During your networking meetings, you will have likely garnered a sense about how they want to achieve their goals and generally what those goals are. Again, this is not a test. You are not an insider, but you do want to be as comprehensive as possible.

In most cases, it is wise to record the desired results in point form for the sake of clarity. The content may look something like this:

- *To achieve a 50/50 commercial / residential mortgage ratio by maintaining current commercial portfolio levels while substantially increasing the residential outstandings.*

- *To streamline administrative activities by centralizing the process in selected centres where optimum cost savings can be achieved.*

- *To maintain current personnel complement numbers over the next two years but to increase staffing in areas directly interfacing with the clients.*

- *To undertake a complete review of demographic trends in an effort to identify the 30 most likely "fast growth" areas between now and the year 2010.*

- *To continue to provide high-quality service to all existing customers.*

- *To reassess the need for the existing network of locations.*

You might feel inclined to include some desired results that seem to be logical extensions of other stated objectives. Tread cautiously. You don't want to put forward an idea that has already been dismissed by the client as inappropriate. As you become more comfortable in your role as a consultant you will find ways to send up some test balloons before you get to the proposal stage. With your first few proposals, keep to the basics unless you feel you are on very firm ground.

OTHER FACTORS TO CONSIDER

This section affords you an opportunity to editorialize, bringing into play the industry research you have gathered, either during your networking or as a result of specifically preparing for the proposal for service.

Your comments might well be linked to some or all of the desired results, and you want to illustrate your additional understanding of factors that may need to be considered. The continuation of the previous example will illustrate how this can be accomplished.

Based on XYZ's last annual report, the outstanding portfolio totalled $ million, with 60% being classified as commercial. If the commercial outstandings are to remain constant and if you wish to achieve a 50/50 ratio between commercial and residential outstandings, this will necessitate an increase in residential volumes of some $ million over the next two years. Given industry projections and current economic forecasts, this will require a larger commitment to the marketing of residential products, likely driven by an expanded and more sophisticated sales force.

To coincidentally meet the objectives of zero growth in the work force, administrative economies of scale will need to be implemented at an early date to allow for personnel complement growth in those areas that will directly contribute to the expansion of the residential mortgage base.

Based on assumptions recently quoted in the June issue of _____, it would appear population growth patterns will be altered in several communities, thereby calling for the re-evaluation of long term business stability in certain areas.

While service to existing clients and communities is critical to sustain market share, the physical presence of a community office may not necessarily be the only means of servicing customers, particularly if the longer term projections for community growth are at levels that may not support the maintenance of a full-fledged office.

Recent technological advances suggest consolidated "back office" operations are becoming much more workable, and earlier legitimate concerns about potential poor service to local clients have been minimized via various direct link-ups with larger, more efficient administrative service centres.

SUGGESTED COURSE OF ACTION AND BENEFITS

In this section you will wish to convey high-level observations followed by your recommended specific action plans. The amount of detail will vary depending upon the type and scope of the assignment.

The following sample does not go into the detailed commentary that would normally flow after each of the recommended action plans. However, in preparing your proposal for service, you will want to explain:

- why each action plan is necessary
- specifically what you will do and when
- what will result

In short, this is where you will outline precisely what the client is going to receive for the money it is spending. This is also where you want to directly link you and your company to the solutions being sought by the client.

Over the course of the past five years, I have been heavily involved in restructuring processes, all aimed at maximizing administrative efficiencies in situations where a company has multiple office locations.

In my opinion, such re-engineering cannot take place in isolation from the rest of the company. Decisions must be predicated upon overall long-term strategies, incorporating a number of issues such as the organization's desired image in the marketplace.

Based on our preliminary discussions, I believe your aggressive objectives can be realized by implementing a co-ordinated plan, including the following components:

- *demographic study of growth areas*
- *analysis of centralization benefits*
- *identification of potential centralized administration sites*
- *implementation of centralization action plans*

As discussed, the first three components of this restructuring need to be finalized and carefully reviewed before moving forward with any implementation strategies.

PROFESSIONAL FEES

In many situations, prospective clients will offer some guidelines on how they prefer to see the fees broken down in a proposal for service. Often companies want to compare the fees of various consultants who are bidding on the same project.

If such guidelines have been suggested, it is always a wise idea to comply. You don't want to cause the company an hour of work attempting to reconfigure your fees to align with the others. You might, however, put forward an alternate fee structure if you believe the client would be impressed with another pricing option.

Above all else, try to keep the pricing straightforward, and precisely record what the client will receive for the recommended fee. If out-of-pocket expenses form part of the fee structure, carefully lay out who pays for what. You don't want to win the contract and then discover you are responsible for all the travel expenses!

The professional fee section might look like this:

With reference to our earlier discussions, pricing in this proposal will be limited to the non-implementation phases. For sake of clarity, we confirm the fees associated with the "Implementation of Centralization Action Plans" will be assessed after the initial studies have been completed and reviewed.

As requested, the breakdown of our fee structure is as follows:

Demographic Study
 7 days @ $1,000 per day — 7,000
Analysis of Centralization Benefits
 5 days @ $1,200 per day — 6,000
Identification of Administrative Sites
 2 days @ $1,200 per day — 2,400

Total — *$15,400*

Please note, the above pricing does not include any allowance for travel expenditures, as you have confirmed all the necessary data is available locally.

We would be in a position to commence this project within 7 days of receiving your approval to proceed.

From time to time, you might want to put forth a proposal without being formally asked to do so. Generally, this occurs after more than one session with a contact and you become aware that the client's needs align with what your company has to offer.

When such a situation arises, you are confronted with the need to take control and actively press forward, thereby developing the opportunity. It is important to recognize not all companies will directly ask for a proposal for service. The onus is often on you to initiate action. They may be waiting to see if you have heard and understood their requirements and if you are assertive enough to act upon their subtle purchasing clues. Indeed, you may be in a position to save the company time and money because they need not search further for a remedy to their problem.

Regardless of what precipitates a proposal for service, there is no guarantee your bid will be accepted. However, a thorough and professional proposal will enhance the probability of landing the contract. At the very least, a well-thought-out proposal for service (even one that does not secure the assignment) will have given you the chance to positively influence your contact for future opportunities, either within their company or outside.

Remember, everything you do will affect your image and reputation. You always have to produce a quality product, because you really don't know who might ultimately become aware of your work.

CHAPTER 13

Activity
The Lost Art of Business Letter Writing

Throughout this book, I have stressed the importance of written communication. Many people question why this seemingly antiquated method of communication is still accentuated. Can we not convey our messages via notes, faxes, e-mails or voice mail? The answer is quite simple. If you want to stand out from your competitors, well written letters can aid you significantly.

Your goal is to set yourself apart from others. An informal yet professionally crafted letter can do just that. Grasp the opportunity to communicate in writing and position yourself on the leading edge, well out in front of the others.

In the next chapter, you will find models of several letters that respond to typical situations but for you to effectively convert these samples for your use, it is important to understand some basic letter writing principles. You need to be cognizant of two primary items: presentation and organization.

PRESENTATION

The presentation section will look at major components that are important if you are to make a favourable impression on the recipient of your letters. These are common sense items but they are worth reviewing to ensure you are achieving the maximum value from every piece of correspondence you dispatch.

PRESENTATION — IMPRESSION

Letters, like people, make a first impression. With a letter detail is a major factor. Let's start with the envelope. The address must be accurate, not handwritten, with the individual addressee clearly identified. If you are sending enclosures, you should definitely be using a large envelope to avoid unnecessary folding of your corporate material.

The letter, on your well-designed letterhead, should be formatted in a businesslike fashion, and print quality should be superior.

PRESENTATION — ACCURACY

All too often, people write great letters, but simple errors and omissions significantly detract from what otherwise may be an outstanding piece of correspondence.

Spelling and grammar must be checked meticulously. Be alert to other factors that could be construed as sensitive issues. In these rapidly changing times, companies are often faced with name changes brought about by mergers and acquisitions. Make certain you use the exact name of the company, including proper punctuation and abbreviations. Companies can have several locations, so double check that your letter is going to reach the recipient at his or her office.

The same care is required in verifying the current title of the person who will receive your letter. Titles change, and many people are extremely sensitive about their official ranking within their organization. Remember, a title denotes position and stature in the company. In many cases individuals have earned the designation through a great deal of personal effort. Show your respect by taking the time to get the title correct.

PRESENTATION — STYLE

Style is an important aspect of good letter writing, and a number of features come into play, not the least of which is your personal writing style. If you try to mimic someone else, it will quickly become evident that you are not the true author of your correspondence. This would also become noticeable during a face-to-face meeting. So be yourself when you write.

Over and above personalizing your letters, there are other issues to consider in terms of overall style. Accent your professionalism by conveying your thoughts in an honest and forthright fashion.

Length is also a factor. While it is important to relay your full message, it is also critical that you respect the time limitations of the recipient. Time is one of the most precious commodities in the business world, and you should always acknowledge that reality in your correspondence.

PRESENTATION — JARGON

Industries, companies and organizations have always invented and used their own jargon, but in the past ten or twenty years, the lexicon of words and phrases has mushroomed. Properly using jargon in your letters can prove to be a very powerful means of demonstrating your familiarity with the business in question. Using incorrect or outdated terminology can illustrate you haven't been keeping pace in an ever-changing business environment.

If you are going to use jargon, use it sparingly, and take the time to make certain you are up on current phrases.

PRESENTATION — FUTURE DIALOGUE

Many letters you write during your marketing efforts will be focused on expanding your network and progressing your relationship with the recipient of your correspondence. In most scenarios, you are attempting to position yourself to tap into other valuable contacts and connections.

Some of the best letter writers fail to leave the door ajar for future opportunities to correspond or meet. It is crucial that your letters specifically address this issue, thereby allowing you to naturally reconnect with contacts as your marketing campaign unfolds.

ORGANIZATION

In almost every company, considerable emphasis is placed upon the ability to be organized and to get things done in a logical and orderly fashion. Organization becomes critical when you are making the effort to acquire new clients. By extension, organization is also a key factor in written communications and the subsequent steps that will flow from your correspondence.

ORGANIZATION — REFERENCING

You are writing letters to effectively showcase yourself and your company to potential clients and to others who might be in a position to assist you in advancing your business.

Most people who receive your letters will be favourably impressed if you accurately record names, dates, places and situations. This attention to detail says something about you as an individual and as a prospective business associate. Look at these examples.

1. "John Smith, the Director of Research at Company B, suggested I give you a call..." is certainly better than "John Smith suggested I call you about..." The recipient of the letter may know four John Smiths.

2. "I wanted to thank you for seeing me on the first of June..." is better than "I wanted to thank you for seeing me." Specifying dates accentuates your attention to detail.

3. "During our conversation you mentioned a new initiative known as *Quality 2000 Plus*..." is much better than "During our conversation you talked about dealing with some service quality issues in the future..." Quoting specifics denotes that you were carefully listening during the conversation.

ORGANIZATION — RESEARCH

One of the cornerstones of running an effective marketing program is research. Proper research can also enhance your written communication skills and set you apart from others.

Once you have established a rapport with an individual, you will want to identify various ways and means of maintaining and cultivating that relationship over the long term. This can be easily accomplished by reconnecting and forwarding material that speaks to topical items of interest.

To do this, you must maintain proper notes about your previous meetings and phone conversations. And you need to keep abreast of other information, including sources like newspapers, periodicals, trade journals and annual reports.

Constant reading and researching will allow you to initiate contact with a good prospect or to maintain a relationship you have already begun to develop.

ORGANIZATION — FOLLOW-UP

Timeliness of follow-up is perhaps one of the best means of demonstrating that you and your company are serious about building a long-term working relationship. If you set a specific time to follow up with a person, meet that commitment. In those cases where you have generalized about follow-up, weigh and consider the best timing and do it!

Maintaining the written portion of your marketing campaign requires personal dedication and it cannot be haphazard. If you do not enjoy writing, it is easy to become distracted. Don't let your letter writing sputter and stall. The following well-worn excuses will not advance your efforts.

- "I've already written this person twice in the past 6 months."
- "It probably wouldn't make any difference."
- "I haven't got time, I've got some other good prospects."
- "I'll do it later."
- "I sent some great follow-up information and I didn't even get a thank-you."

Successful marketers and networkers carefully maintain their written communications.

CHAPTER 14

Activity
Business Writing — Examples and Explanations

I have intentionally avoided pro formas. Providing fill-in-the-blank forms and letters has a habit of sapping originality and creativity, which are so vital if you want to set yourself apart from others.

The following approach to written communications will supply you with some good examples. More important, the explanatory notes will offer you insight as to what you should be striving for when you take the time to design a well-constructed piece of correspondence. As you read the balance of this chapter I would encourage you to visualize how you might effectively re-tool these items to suit your own purposes.

#1 NETWORKING SET-UP LETTER —
REFERENCING A BUSINESS ASSOCIATE
Explanatory Notes

This is a direct form of introductory communication, but it does have the distinct advantage of referring to a mutual business acquaintance. Elements worth noting:

- The letter is short and to the point.
- The second paragraph indicates your area of specialization and your main services.

- Paragraph three honestly concedes you are a newcomer. It also accents that rather than blatantly selling your services, you are seeking information.
- You acknowledge that the recipient is busy and you confirm what future action you will be taking.
- By modifying the first paragraph, this letter is easily adapted to situations where you do not have an introductory reference.

We have not met but Jane Willis from XYZ Inc. suggested I should contact you regarding our financial and retirement planning consulting services.

Just by way of a brief background, our group concentrates solely on retirement planning for employees of major corporations. We not only offer the more traditional financial planning services but we also provide support through our pre-retirement counselling programs, which are directed toward employees and spouses who will soon want to make informed decisions concerning various aspects of retirement life.

As a relative newcomer to this field we have not had an opportunity to deal with your company. With this in mind, I would like to speak with you regarding the criteria you utilize in selecting this type of consulting support.

I appreciate your schedule is hectic but I will endeavour to contact you by phone during the week of June eight and perhaps we can arrange a short introductory meeting.

#2 NETWORKING SET-UP LETTER — RESEARCH
Explanatory notes

This was perhaps the most successful letter I used when launching my re-employment counselling business. A number of elements deserve attention.

- The recipient can immediately identify and agree with the statements in the first two paragraphs. You want affirmative nodding as they scan the start of the letter.

- The third paragraph spells out precisely the business focus of your organization, without any specific sales pitch.

- Paragraph four clearly states what you want to achieve by meeting with the target contact. You want to discuss some topics of mutual interest. You are not seeking a meeting to sell the recipient something.

- The close is important. You do want to acknowledge the person is busy but you also want to specifically lay out the course of action you intend to take.

Without doubt the upcoming two or three years will continue to present unparalleled challenges to the ABC industry and meeting operating objectives will hinge on a number of factors including:

- a reassessment of marketing strategies
- a careful analysis of operating procedures
- an in-depth review of customer expectations
- a dedication to sound management practices

These key ingredients share a common element — the effective management of Human Resources. As successful executives move forward in this era of unprecedented change, they will be faced with critical decisions concerning the optimum utilization of their people.

Our recently established firm is dedicated to being a strategic partner to businesses, supplying customized Human Resource Consulting to meet the specific needs of clients in transition. We concentrate solely on providing specialized re-employment counselling to senior employees.

As part of our commitment to responding to the future expectations of corporate clients, we like to meet with organizations to discuss issues such as:

- How you select Human Resource consultants.
- What service components & standards are most critical.
- How you measure the success of such assignments.

While I recognize your time is at a premium, I will be in touch by phone during the week of August seventeenth, and perhaps we can arrange a mutually convenient meeting to review these topics. I look forward to speaking with you in the not too distant future.

#3 CONGRATULATIONS —
A NEWLY APPOINTED PERSON
Explanatory Notes

Admittedly, this letter employs a much more subtle approach. Advantages or uses:

- You may already be networking with one of the recipient's associates. The letter is common courtesy. You might start the letter by saying, "Bill Smith from your office informed me of your arrival and I wanted..." This phrase immediately links you to the company.
- The second paragraph states the obvious, but without going into detail you explain what you do and make the offer to provide assistance.
- The letter positions you for a subsequent call, during which you can refer to your congratulatory letter.
- Congratulatory letters are uncommon. By sending one, you are setting yourself apart from others. I sent one to a newly appointed HR person who did not receive a welcome from the consulting firm her company had used in the past. As you might expect, she was more impressed with yours truly.

I simply wanted to take this opportunity to congratulate you on your recent appointment as the Director of Marketing.

Based on our heavy involvement with all segments of the food services industry, I can fully appreciate the many challenges on the horizon as you assume your new responsibilities. Certainly if we can be of any assistance in our capacity as market research consultants, please don't hesitate to get in touch with my office.

I look forward to meeting you at some point in the future and again, every success in your new endeavours.

#4 FOLLOW-UP MARKETING LETTER — REFERENCING A NEWS ITEM
Explanatory Notes

The writer of this letter has been quoted in a magazine, and the content of the article is generic enough that it can be sent to a wide range of clients. Other points:

- The opening is informal. Every recipient will agree with the statement about being busy.
- Paragraph two is generic and it can be used universally. You come across as humbly proud that you were involved in the preparation of the article.
- The last paragraph includes a general follow-up commitment. The letter was written solely as a means of keeping in touch with a large client base. The writer probably felt he or she would have spare time later in the summer to establish phone or personal contact.
- This is a great way to manage your marketing campaign but you do have to meet even the vaguest deadlines you have imposed upon yourself.

I expect your schedule has not slowed since our last exchange of calls and I thought it might be better to drop you a quick note.

Given the ongoing changes we are all facing, I felt you may find the enclosed item from Air Canada's *En Route* magazine to be of interest. We were fortunate to be involved in the preparation of the article and as you might anticipate, there was considerable debate about the various topics.

Carrie, I will endeavour to reconnect by phone later in the summer. If we can be of any assistance between now and then, please give me a call.

#5 FOLLOW-UP TO A NETWORKING MEETING
Explanatory Notes

I am not a big advocate of leaving promotional materials with a contact at the end of a meeting. By forwarding your information after the fact, you have yet another vehicle to favourably impress the person. The main features:

- Be timely in dispatching the letter — no more than a day after your meeting. Record the date of the meeting to emphasize your attention to detail.
- The phrase "as promised" reinforces that you keep your commitments.
- Your mission statement is optional. It can be a good way to synthesize what you do and how you go about doing it.
- The next paragraph repeats what you do, while accenting the core components of your business. Let your corporate brochure provide the expanded version.
- It's a good idea to develop a stock letter flexible enough to let you add paragraphs as needed. This allows you to respond to specifics you may have discussed. By crafting commonly used

correspondence in this fashion, you achieve efficiency, while retaining a customized feel.

- The last paragraph keeps the door ajar for ongoing dialogue.

Thank you for taking the time to see me on the thirteenth of March. I appreciated your candid comments and observations.

As promised, I am enclosing some material that will give you a sense of our values and an outline of the various translation services offered by our firm. We are often asked what differentiates us from our competitors, and that is a fair question. Our response can best be summarized by our mission statement:

Insert Mission Statement

While we are equipped to handle a full range of translation assignments, our primary focus is on the Central and South American markets. We also offer personalized tutoring for executives who wish to learn or upgrade their foreign language skills. When your office is faced with a need for this type of support, we would be pleased to discuss your requirements more fully.

Insert Paragraph Dealing With Items Discussed

Jack, I would like to thank you for taking the time to review our material. As agreed, I will be in touch periodically to keep apprised of any changes within your organization.

#6 FOLLOW-UP MARKETING LETTER — NO PHONE REPLY
Explanatory Notes

Not all your well crafted letters are going to result in a response to your request for a meeting. Indeed, on some occasions your elusive contact will not even return your phone calls. Don't try to guess why

— remember, you may have run into someone who only communicates when there is a reason. This is not the time to write off the contact. Here are a few notes concerning the following letter:

- The opening paragraph is intended to make two points. First, you are following through as you said you would, although your contact has failed to return your calls. Second, you refer to your initial correspondence on the off chance that the contact has failed to make the connection between the letter and your subsequent phone calls.
- It is not coincidental that letters 5 and 6 are similar. A few minor alterations will make one letter easily fit another situation. Take the example a step further. Either of these two letters could be adapted to a situation where you did not meet someone in person, but you had a phone conversation.
- The start of paragraph two offers the recipient a graceful out. You are positioning yourself for a more positive response when you next call.
- The last paragraph is nothing more than further positioning on your part to set the stage for a future call. You have also offered to answer any questions arising from your material.

I wanted to follow up on my recent efforts to reach you by phone and my earlier correspondence dating back to the sixteenth of November.

Recognizing that your schedule is undoubtedly very hectic, I thought perhaps it may be more expedient to forward you some material, which will give you a sense of our values and an outline of the various translation services offered by our firm. We are often asked what differentiates us from our competitors, and that is a fair question. Our response can best be summarized by our mission statement:

Insert Mission Statement

While we are equipped to handle a full range of translation assignments, our primary focus is on the Central and South American markets. We also offer personalized tutoring for executives who wish to learn or upgrade their foreign language skills. When your office is faced with a need for this type of support, we would be pleased to discuss your requirements more fully.

Susan, I would like to thank you for reviewing our material and I will make an effort to reconnect with you during the first week of December.

In the meantime, if you have any questions, please give me a call.

#7 FOLLOW-UP MARKETING LETTER — SUPPLYING INFORMATION
Explanatory Notes

This type of letter can be dispatched to both prospective and existing clients. Over and above being an easy means of keeping in contact, the letter also offers the following advantages:

- The first paragraph reasserts your line of business. Some recipients will be well known to you and restating your purpose in life might not be necessary. In other instances, new prospects may need a reminder about what you do.
- The referenced article has two major advantages. First, it is generally applicable to your line of consulting. Second, it comes from a well respected source. Not only are you imparting useful information, but you are also making a subtle statement concerning how your company keeps current.
- Your final paragraph paves the way to a follow-up call. It is casual, but it also implies you are cognizant how hectic the summer vacation season can be for those who work for a large company.

As you will appreciate, much of our corporate re-engineering work stems directly from the re-organization efforts of our clients and in most situations, we are involved in the planning stages.

During a recent restructuring project, we happened to make reference to an item entitled "Informal Networks: The Company Behind the Chart" which appeared in the *Harvard Business Review*. Our client was intrigued by this additional dimension. If you have not already had an opportunity to review this article I thought you might find the attached reprint to be informative.

Lynda, if we can be of any assistance in the future, please give me a call and I will make an effort to reconnect with you as soon as the summer vacation season is over.

#8 FOLLOW-UP MARKETING LETTER —
REFERENCING A NEW SERVICE
Explanatory Notes

This letter accomplishes two goals. You are imparting information that is of interest to your clients and you are assisting an associate by transmitting data about their product or service. This is good for all concerned. Notable highlights:

- The first and second paragraphs give the reader a glimpse of how you conduct business and what makes you different.
- Paragraph three stresses your ongoing efforts to seek out new and innovative ways of providing up-to-date support. The commentary also formally announces the expanded service, supplemented by some informative data about the affiliate.
- The penultimate paragraph provides tangible information, which will be of interest to the reader. By reviewing the material, the client has a better understanding of how your efforts will directly assist them.

- The past paragraph is an open invitation for a client to follow up with you. No high pressure, just a genuine passing comment to stress you are there to help.

As you will recall from our information brochure, all finalists in our recruitment process are given one or more forms of personal assessment before the candidate files are passed on to our corporate clients. This applies to both management and non-management assignments.

We strongly believe this is one of the critical steps in assisting our corporate clients in reaching an informed decision relative to the selection of the right person for the position in question.

For the past year, we have been investigating new assessment options and we have recently concluded arrangements with Thomas International Management Systems. Thomas has been providing behavioral evaluations since 1926 and they have a global network of some 50 offices in 34 countries. We are pleased to announce that we are now officially licensed to administer this assessment vehicle.

In an effort to keep you informed, we are enclosing a sample of the output from a typical Thomas assessment. We are confident you will find this type of information to be an invaluable aid when deliberating over the short list of potential job candidates we put forward.

Should you have any specific questions concerning the Thomas or if you have any general enquiries, please give me a call.

#9 FOLLOW-UP MARKETING LETTER —
UPDATE ON CHANGES
Explanatory Notes

This sample letter is much more targeted to certain corporations. Items worth noting:

- The opening paragraph re-establishes contact by specifying your field of expertise. Your attention to detail is underscored via quoting when you last provided a Corporate Review.
- Paragraph two zeroes in on new features.
- The last paragraph sets forth your intended course of action.
- This letter could be adapted to go with a mass mailing of your revised corporate review.

Over the course of the past year, we had an opportunity to speak on a few occasions about our public relations consulting services. Based on my records, I provided you with a copy of our Corporate Review in July of last year.

Since then, we have experienced several changes within our group — including the addition of another local partner and the establishment of formal affiliate arrangements with a firm in Vancouver. We have also made some changes to the services we offer. I thought it would be appropriate to forward a revised version of our material.

Dave, given the changes in our organization it may be timely to review some of the issues we discussed during our first meeting. I will endeavour to connect with you in the first week of September.

#11 ANNOUNCEMENT — EXPANDING SERVICES
Explanatory Notes

In time, you may find yourself expanding your business beyond the geographic boundaries you had originally established. Take a look at the following example:

- A simple announcement can be beneficial to your company. The mailing will be inexpensive if you use your letterhead.
- The announcement immediately conveys a positive image — expansion is automatically associated with progress.

- By inserting the last paragraph you maintain control to make certain your existing clients are being properly introduced to your partner in Montreal and your new affiliates.
- When next printing letterhead, incorporate a notation about the Montreal office and your Western affiliations.

WE ARE PLEASED TO ANNOUNCE.....

.... Ms. Maria LeSalle has become the Managing Partner for our Quebec operation and we have simultaneously relocated our Montreal offices to expanded facilities at:

900 boul Levesque East, Suite 5450
Montreal, Quebec H5L 3L9

In a further effort to provide our corporate clients with greater accessibility to personalized desktop publishing services in Western Canada, we would also like to take this opportunity to inform you we have established affiliates in Vancouver and Calgary.

If you encounter situations where you require our support in any of these areas, please give me a call. I would be happy to coordinate all the necessary activities or arrange for the appropriate introductions.

11 FOLLOW-UP MARKETING LETTER —
REFERENCING A BOOK
Explanatory Notes

This letter was taken directly from one of the marketing initiatives I used in a former life. Notwithstanding the rather self-serving references, you will see the advantages connected to using your own publication as a marketing tool. Additional notes:
- Writing and publishing a book will have the added advantage of driving down the cost of such a giveaway item.

- Assuming the book relates to your business endeavours, there is a definite benefit to being published. Presumably not all your competitors can make the same claim.
- Publishing a book affords you access to public speaking engagements, which will heighten your marketplace image.
- This is not the route for every consultant, but most who have taken the plunge into writing acknowledge the benefits.

Last year we announced the publication of *From Fired... ....To Hired.*

There were several reasons behind writing the book. Based on market research, we discovered a significant demand from the public at large for a pragmatic guide to aid those job-seekers who did not enjoy the support of re-employment counselling via their previous employer.

Also, we wanted to augment our existing comprehensive material to further assist our individual clients and their families in grasping the full spectrum of initiatives required to conduct a successful career transition. Lastly, many of our corporate clients had been asking for information that would allow them to better understand the rigors associated with the job search process.

As always, we like to keep you informed about the enhancements we are introducing and I trust you will find the enclosed second edition of the book to be both informative and thought provoking.

Dean, if you are faced with any requirements for re-employment counselling support in the future, we would welcome the opportunity to offer our assistance.

#12 ANNOUNCEMENT — BUSINESS OPENING
Explanatory Notes

Many small first time businesses fail to send out any type of opening announcement. Based on my discussions with several new entrepreneurs I think the reason stems from the fact they have no real clients to communicate with, so they don't send out anything. Consider the following:

- Announce your opening to everyone you know — even friends, relatives and previous business associates.
- The announcement formalizes the opening and gives you the opportunity to forward your business card.
- Announcements can be formally printed but it can be just as effective to send the information on your new letterhead.
- Noting the web site address is another means of creating a positive image relative to this small accounting firm.
- No need to sign the announcements. In this example, Ryan's name appears at the bottom to facilitate the inclusion of his CA designation.

WE ARE PLEASED TO ANNOUNCE.....

.....................the formal opening of GTP Accounting Inc., effective March 1st. GTP will be concentrating on providing a comprehensive range of accounting services to individuals and small businesses in Calgary and the surrounding area. Our office is located at:

> 145 Edge Hill Mount - #14
> Calgary, Alberta
> T2P 101

We look forward to serving you in the future and if we can be of any assistance, please contact us by phone at 403-555-1212 or by fax at 403-555-1200.

See our web site (www.cafouru.com) for more details.

> Ryan Potter CA

#13 FOLLOW-UP MARKETING LETTER —
PROVIDING NEW INFORMATION
Explanatory Notes

The following is another example of a letter that can be forwarded to existing and potential clients to keep them informed about things you are doing. Note:

- Clients always appreciate receiving information. By supplying interesting and timely material, you develop a reputation, linking you to quality information.

- This letter is very generic in nature. You could easily use it as a direct mailer to all clients, particularly on those occasions when you are too busy to follow up personally by phone.

- Keep your eyes open for information suitable to your marketing endeavours. You might not be able to use it today, but it could come in handy six months from now.

Over the course of the past five years, employment trends have shifted dramatically.

As consultants to small businesses we have seen an increased demand from prospective individual clients to assist them in investigating the start-up or purchase of a business venture.

Self-employment endeavours can prove to be a good choice but careful research is an essential ingredient in the decision-making process. To aid our new clients in their initial deliberations we frequently refer them to an authoritative reference source, which is entitled **First Steps — A Guide to Starting a Business in Ontario.**

In an effort to keep you apprised of the leading edge material we are utilizing, we wanted to provide you with a copy of the above mentioned publication. We gratefully acknowledge Smith Nixon, Chartered Accountants for supplying the enclosed edition.

Should you have any questions about our small business consulting services, please give me a call. We would welcome the opportunity to discuss your future requirements.

Armed with this information we will move forward to investigate how you can put some of these writing ideas into practical use through your ongoing marketing and networking endeavours.

CHAPTER 15

Activity
Ongoing Marketing and Networking

During the start-up of any company, we all learn a number of lessons. Perhaps the toughest one is never to stop marketing and networking, even when you are in the enviable position of enjoying good business fortunes.

Achieving a balance between working for a fee and working toward securing the next contract is difficult at the best of times. It is even more taxing if you are a one-person operation. It is easy to become distracted when you are juggling paying clients, posting invoices, proof reading a new advertising pamphlet, and attending an important lecture.

There is a solution to the dilemma if you have the discipline to keep organized. Being organized is an absolute must if you want to succeed in the consulting business. If you are not naturally well-organized, seek professional help.

With a little forward planning, you can maintain contact with existing and prospective clients even when you are in the midst of a major assignment. If you think back to the chapter on marketing plans, you may recall the suggestion to specify exactly what you envision doing to keep yourself prominently in front of clients. Timing of these marketing interventions was also discussed. Learn to work the plan and abide by the commitments you made to yourself.

MAINTAINING CONTACT WITH CLIENTS

A plan can be easily set in motion. Let's walk through a scenario that outlines possible marketing interventions for one year.

1. introductory letter
2. follow-up phone call to secure networking meeting
3. another call because the first one went unanswered
4. networking meeting
5. follow up with your brochure
6. dispatch of relevant trade journal article
7. follow-up phone call to stress interest in business
8. forward a news item in which you are quoted
9. Christmas / Season's Greetings cards sent to all clients
10. phone call in the New Year to discuss future plans
11. send annual copy of your brochure

The foregoing is by no means an outlandish example of what you might do with each and every one of your prospective clients during a twelve-month period. Indeed, in many cases, the same marketing interventions can apply to existing customers.

Information Mailings

Some will argue that it is impossible to keep up such an intensive campaign if you are also regularly working with paying clients. But take the time to consider items 6 and 8. Your biggest challenge will be to select what material to send. Then it is a matter of crafting one marketing letter, which can be sent to everyone in your client data base.

To make your life even easier, a good data base will allow you to design a stock letter that includes the recipient's name in the body of the letter to add that personal touch. This is why you only use a contact's preferred name in a data base. You don't want to send a letter recording Ed in one part and Edward in another section of the correspondence. Chalk that pointer up to one of my personal mistakes when initially setting up my own data base!

Season's Greetings

You will notice that Christmas / Season's Greetings cards have been included as a means of contact. I suppose you can debate the appropriateness of sending cards because not all of your clients will be celebrating the Christmas holiday. Personally, I tend to look at Christmas in the broader context — a holiday that is widely observed throughout North America. You can certainly purchase nondenominational cards that stress the Season's Greetings aspect and good wishes for the New Year.

If you are going to go to the expense of sending cards and if you want them to partially act as a marketing intervention, there are a few pointers to remember. Don't be cheap. Purchase a good quality card, one that is unique and eye-catching. You want people to pause to admire your choice. There is nothing wrong with having your company name embossed on the inside of the card, but take the time to personally sign it. If you are not going to sign the cards, don't bother buying them. Remember your image. You want to accentuate the personal aspect.

Items 6, 8 and 9 are all marketing interventions, which can be easily accomplished with a minimal expenditure of time — if you are organized.

Phone Calls

The two commitments to make phone calls are more labour intensive, but they are important. Your first objective is to keep in touch, and your second is to confirm that the person is still there. If you reach a new person, you will have some further investigations to conduct to determine what has transpired since your last meeting or phone conversation.

If your original contact has moved on to another company, follow up and reconnect. This is a great opportunity to expand your network. Also, instigate action to introduce yourself to the person who took over from your original contact.

When it comes to making telephone calls, I like to carve out a couple of days during slow periods and concentrate on nothing but making those calls. Getting the task done in a relatively short time is perhaps the best way to motivate yourself, rather than dragging out the calling process over several days.

Taking the time to call a contact is almost as important as actually reaching the individual. If you reach the person when you call, so much the better, because you can advance your keen desire to do business. But even if you end up in the voice mail vortex, you have an opportunity to keep up your relationship. Your message might go something like this:

"Jane, it is Reg Pirie calling from Ink Ink Publishing. It is Tuesday, about 9:30. I was just phoning to update you on a couple of new initiatives we are introducing. I appreciate you are extremely busy but if you have a moment, perhaps you could give me a call back at 555-4321. Look forward to catching up with you later."

If you are not currently up to your ears in work, you can call Jane back in a week if she has not responded to the original message.

Corporate Brochures

You will note from the previous list of possible interventions that the last item recorded is the dispatch of another brochure. This warrants an explanation. Approximately once a year you will want to consider sending out a fresh copy of your promotional material, even if there has not been a significant change in the content. Why? As much as we would all like to think our clients keep our material close at hand, the truth is that over the course of a year it has likely been misplaced, filed incorrectly or discarded in the annual office cleanup.

During the first few years of your operation, there might be some legitimate changes in your material. If so, your covering letter should highlight the alterations.

OTHER MEANS OF KEEPING IN TOUCH

In the next few pages you will find some additional marketing intervention suggestions that may prove helpful if you think you have exhausted all other avenues. I have used this part of the book as a catch-all in an effort to pass along some thoughts, experiences and observations I have gleaned in my years as a consultant.

Breakfast Meetings

Because of the expense, this is a marketing idea you may wish to reserve for year two of your operation. Generally the reason for the gathering is to pass along topical information to clients via a qualified guest speaker. You might have to pay the speaker, or it might be an old associate who is willing to barter his or her services for some of your time.

Such an event affords you more than one marketing opportunity. The first intervention is the invitation, which should go to everyone in your data base. Don't worry about being oversubscribed. If you are, you can apologize while stating the response has been phenomenal. Those who are turned aside will think they have missed out on a great presentation. The second is the breakfast itself. Here are a few tips to consider as you prepare to host a breakfast meeting:

- Select a reasonably central location
- Choose a good-quality hotel or other such establishment
- Set a start time that is early but not too early
- Send the invitations out well in advance

- Ask for a reply by a specified time
- Limit the number of attendees to no more than twenty-five — remember, you want to chat with each guest
- Have name tags available for the convenience of your guests
- Stay on schedule — guests have other appointments
- Follow up with a thank-you for attending

No, breakfast meetings are not for everyone. If you do find them to be an effective venue, limit such gatherings to once or twice a year. You might want to start an annual gathering associated with some other major event.

One of my colleagues hosts a breakfast every January to offer his clients some insights into what the new year will bring. Another associate times his annual breakfast for a week or two after RRSP season ends. He provides consultative services to the financial planning community, and the meeting affords a great opportunity to share information.

Announcements

Announcements that convey information to your clients are a fast, easy and effective way to maintain your presence in the marketplace. You do not necessarily need to send a personalized letter. Your printer can mass produce a quality announcement and that leaves you with the relatively simple task of running mailing labels and stuffing envelopes. The postage meter comes in handy when you have 500 pieces of mail to dispatch. If you are too busy to stuff envelopes, enlist the help of your children or a favourite niece who wants to earn some money.

By the way, treat announcements as a marketing intervention to keep your company name in front of clients. I once knew a consultant who vainly tried to cost justify mailing an announcement to say his firm had opened a web site. The decision almost drove him crazy because he could not quantify what he might reap by way of a tangible payback. In these circumstances there is no measurable or immediate reward. You are simply enhancing and expanding your image.

Lunches

I still run into some consultants who think buying a client a lunch will somehow magically generate a sale. After years as a corporate employee I grew to detest the "free" business lunch, because I spent the entire meal waiting for the sales pitch.

Lunches are not for selling. Lunches are social events where you can get to know your contact on a more personal level. I go out of my way to avoid talking about business at lunch. If your guest brings up business issues, fine. If not, enjoy a time-out from your hectic pace and get to know your contact a little better. A casual lunch will stand you in much better stead with a client than a meeting over a meal where you flog your services.

Free Tickets

From time to time you will discover you are the recipient of free tickets or passes to business or social events. For whatever reason, I always seem to end up with a dozen free passes to the local mall business show. Distribute such items to select clients. It is the gesture that counts, even if they don't attend the function.

In other scenarios you might be given complimentary tickets to a seminar where you are one of the guest speakers. Again, use those freebies and pass them along to clients.

Newsletters

Many consulting firms effectively use newsletters to communicate on a regular basis with potential and existing clients. If the newsletter is consistently superior and if the information is germane to your readers, this is a great way to stay in touch.

However, a couple of major drawbacks warrant comment. Many consultants introduce newsletters during the start-up of their companies, when they have the time to devote to the undertaking. The first issues seem to be easy to produce, but as you get busier, a newsletter can become a burden.

This problem can be exacerbated if you made a commitment to supply the publication on a scheduled basis. Over and above the time commitment you might also discover that finding material for each edition is a more difficult as time progresses.

Give the subject some serious thought before you leap into print.

Surveys

Conducting surveys and imparting the results to your clients can be a great marketing tool. But like deciding to produce a newsletter, this venture requires some careful deliberation and investigation, particularly if surveys are not within your own area of expertise.

My advice is to seek someone who has conducted one or two simplistic surveys in the past and find out what is involved. If those discussions lead you to believe this is something you can do yourself, by all means go ahead.

If you are planning a more sophisticated survey that requires the design of measurement applications, secure professional assistance through a firm like Organizational Studies International, Inc., an acknowledged leader in this field. Such companies can formulate survey questionnaires to maximize the output you eventually receive.

Vacation Announcements

One last marketing intervention idea, which can place you in a positive light with existing clients. If you are a one-person operation, you are eventually going to need a break from the action before total burnout occurs. Yes, even consultants get to take a few days off to recharge!

You can turn your vacation into an image-enhancing undertaking. I am not suggesting you communicate your vacation schedule to all the prospects in your data base. However, it makes good sense to drop a note or even a voice mail message to those clients who have used your services in the past year.

By doing this you set yourself apart from many other consultants, who don't make the effort to pass along this type of information. They are the ones who leave a voice mail on their machines saying they will be back in a week and then they hope their clients don't call with an assignment while they are vacationing.

If you let people know in advance, they have time to connect with you to arrange for a meeting immediately before or after your time off. If you are doing a good job for your clients, most will try to be accommodating when you are attempting to get away for a short vacation.

Much earlier in this book I put forth the hypothesis that the truly successful independent consultant is the person who genuinely embraces and enjoys all aspects of networking and marketing. Few of us are born to network and market. On the other hand, with some diligent effort, most of us can learn how to generate and initiate those ideas that will drive our ventures forward.

The networking and marketing suggestions contained in this and other chapters are only a few examples of how to effectively position yourself and your company for the future. Start by using some of these proven methods and then slowly develop your own strategies. For those who are determined and persistent, networking will become a state of mind.

CHAPTER 16

Focus, Organization, Research and Activity
Developing a Business Plan

There are a few reasons the business plan chapter is in the back of this book. Since I am one of those authors who tends to write from page one to the end of a manuscript, I always find a way to procrastinate or rationalize why my least favourite topic should be hidden near the last section. The subject of preparing a business plan falls in that category.

From a more practical standpoint, I believe tackling a business plan is not easily done unless you have a well-rounded overview of the entire picture. The last fifteen chapters have, I hope, provided you with the necessary broad perspective. Without doubt, taking the time to complete a formal business plan is a wise idea. If for no other reason, preparing the plan provides a structure that allows you to reflect on issues you may not have fully considered before.

In the event you have an immediate need or an anticipated need for financing, a business plan will be a high priority with your banker. Should you be looking at financing from other sources like an investor, the plan will also be essential.

Business plans fall into two main groupings: the abbreviated ones, which are nearly useless, and the massive ones, which are almost overkill. Since this book is primarily targeted at the small independent consultant, an attempt has been made to achieve a balance.

We will look at four main topics: Information Summary, Market Assessment, Marketing & Operational Plans and Financial Overview & Projections. When writing your plan, bear in mind the purpose is to justify and illustrate how you will succeed, supported by:

- details of your company
- an outline of your research and your target market, including why targeted clients will buy from you
- an explanation of your services, including how you intend to attract new clients and retain the old ones
- explanatory notes concerning financial matters, backed up by financial and statistical data to support your projections

INFORMATION SUMMARY

BUSINESS PLAN
INFORMATION SUMMARY

Company Name, Address and Contact Numbers
Type of Company
Names of Officers / Partners
Nature of Business
Professional Support Team

Company Name, Address and Contact Numbers

This is self-explanatory but provide all current information.

Type of Company

Indicate incorporated, sole ownership or partnership. If you are in the midst of incorporating, record the details.

Names of Officers / Partners etc.

Note all names in full, home addresses and for incorporated entities, the title held by each company officer.

Nature of Business

Include a summary of the nature of your business and an overview of the services offered.

Professional Support Team

List all members of your team, including accountant, lawyer, financial planner, banker, insurance agent, insurance broker and other appropriate individuals. It is helpful to include company names, addresses and phone and fax numbers.

MARKET ASSESSMENT

BUSINESS PLAN
MARKET ASSESSMENT

Historical Review of Industry
Assessment of Industry Future
Overview of Major Competitors
Differentiating Factors
Target Market

Historical Review of Industry

Offer your reader a sense of what has previously transpired in your chosen field of endeavour. This section serves to clearly demonstrate that you have done your homework in terms of assessing trends and how those historical factors could influence the future.

Assessment of Industry Future

Springboarding off the previous item, you will want to outline where your industry is headed, both in the short-term and the long-term. If there are significant influencing factors, these should be recorded and substantiated by referring to your research material and other sources.

Pay particular attention to key factors such as: technological advancements, economic implications, government regulations and de-regulations, shifting market trends, general growth patterns and changing client requirements. Last, but by no means least, address why there will be a sustained demand for the services you offer.

Overview of Major Competitors

Most of us are fully convinced we can build a better mousetrap. Notwithstanding that belief, your overview of major competitors will be of critical interest to the readers of your business plan. You will need to convey that you are completely familiar with how your competition does business. Note what they do well, and also comment on those areas where they are not meeting the changing requirements of the marketplace.

Differentiating Factors

What makes my company notably different? Why do I think I can compete with established firms? What new products or services will I introduce to win out over my competitors? Will my methods and service distinguish me from others? What changes will I need to make in the future to maintain a leading edge?

These questions, and a host of others, should be addressed in a comprehensive fashion. The good news is that most of this material can be drawn from the work you have already done when preparing your marketing plan.

Target Market

If you have done a thorough job of completing your marketing plan, this section is a recap of what or who you plan to target, and why. For more details, the reader of your business plan can be referred to the commentary under Marketing & Operational Plans — Key Areas of Marketing Concentration.

MARKETING / OPERATIONAL PLANS

BUSINESS PLAN
MARKETING / OPERATIONAL PLANS

Scope of Services
Principles, Values, Guarantees
Methodologies and Differentiating Factors
Geographic Boundaries
Service Providers and Qualifications
Key Areas of Marketing Concentration
Marketing Philosophy
Specific Marketing Action Plans
References
Operational Considerations
• Office Space/Location
• Fixed Assets
• Accounting
• Legal Issues
• Insurance — Property Coverage
• Administration
• Others

With the exception of references and operational considerations, all the headings in this section have been covered in detail during the chapter nine review of how to develop a marketing plan. It would be prudent to cut and paste the data into your formal business plan. It is easier to do it now rather than six months down the road when you unexpectedly need a formal business plan to convince your banker that you are a good credit risk.

References

This issue was covered previously. It does bear repeating in a business plan as the readers of your plan will want to know how potential clients can confirm your qualifications.

Operational Considerations

This heading may appear to be a catchall and perhaps it is. However, the so-called sundry items warrant explanation in your business plan, and the scope of this section might include answers to or comments about the following:

- Is this a home-based business operation and why will it work from that type of venue?
- If the business is home-based, are there pre-determined thresholds that will cause you to expand? If so, where will you expand?
- In the event you are using an executive office facility, what services are provided?
- Describe the longevity of existing equipment. Future equipment needs may deserve comment, if technology is a major component of your business.
- Record how day-to-day accounting matters will be handled, and by whom.
- If your line of business typically signs formal contracts, what format will you be using? Have these documents been vetted by your lawyer?
- What insurance coverage is in place for fixed assets?
- If your business is administratively intense, who will handle these matters? How is your admin person qualified?

FINANCIAL OVERVIEW AND PROJECTIONS

This is where most business plans come to a grinding halt. Why? Because the vast majority of us do not understand finances, or we choose not to understand them. When you think about it, the situation is almost comical. The one thing so many of us hate to handle is likely the single most important item in determining the success of a business.

It may sound like I am being very flippant about this subject but indeed I am not. I have seen far too many businesses fail because the owners did not pay attention to money matters. Stop here, go back to chapter four and re-read the first six or seven pages. The reason for asking you to take this detour is to help you decide how much assistance you require in properly developing this portion of your business plan.

The financial section is far too important for you to gloss over it, just because you don't like dealing with financial issues. The consequences of making a mistake can be far reaching. You want to make certain you have enough money to start up your company. You don't want to create future tax problems. You don't want to be so poorly prepared that you can't explain and justify your requirements to your banker.

Personally I would suggest it is prudent for most independent consultants to ask an accountant for assistance in preparing the numbers part of the financial projections portion of the business plan. You will still be responsible for pulling together the raw data and the supporting material. The figures can then be assembled in the four primary financial statements:

- Personal Financial Statements
- Opening Balance Sheet
- Projected Income and Expense Statement *
- Cash Flow Projection *

Once the preliminary statements are prepared, sit down with your accountant and review the information so you fully understand all the implications. The two statements marked with an asterisk are only projections, but you should have a reasonable sense of whether you are going to require operating loans to finance receivables. This is also the time to discuss the financing of any major capital expenditures — either immediate needs, or those within the first twelve months of operation.

Assuming your accountant does the number crunching, you will still need to know the answers to many questions. In essence, the following headings will assist you in gathering the correct information to input to the statements and in preparing the written material for your business plan.

BUSINESS PLAN
FINANCIAL OVERVIEW AND PROJECTIONS

Personal Financial Statements

Opening Balance Sheet

Projected Income and Expense Statement
- Projected Income (Contracts / Work In Progress)
- Expenses

Cash Flow Projection
- Aged Account Receivables

Request for Loan Accommodation

Term loans
- Purpose (Description of Asset to be Purchased and Cost)
- Loan Amount Requested
- Justification for Capital Expenditure

- Down Payment (Equity)
- Repayment Schedule
- Security Offered

Operating loan
- Purpose
- Loan Amount Requested
- Repayment Schedule
- Security Offered

Personal Financial Statements

Why I am leading off with this item when we are dealing with a business plan? Because the majority of independent consulting businesses are funded in whole or in part by personal resources.

Most of us have relatively straightforward personal financial statements and your accountant should be able to highlight any anomalies that warrant mention in the explanatory notes of your business plan. Your personal statements are important.

Company Opening Balance Sheet

This is the starting point of a company's financial reporting. If this is day one of your company's existence, the entries will be minimal. Assets might include personal furnishings and equipment you have sold to the company. The liabilities might be loans from shareholders — the cash you have injected in to the company for start-up purposes.

Company Projected Income and Expense Statement

This is the key document. Given my neophyte status when it comes to financial matters, my accountant likes to say this form estimates what will come in and what will go out! As you might expect, it is always more difficult to estimate the income side.

Income

This section should include your income (sales) estimates for the year, supplemented by a commentary on when such income might occur. You will want to make suitable comments about your pricing and fee structure to substantiate your estimates. If your company is apt to have income from other sources, this too should be noted and explained.

If you are fortunate enough to have a signed contracts or work in progress at the time of preparing your business plan, these noteworthy items deserve comment and explanation.

Expenses

Your accountant will want to categorize your expenses in two or three different groupings. Let the accountant worry about that. Your main concern is to carefully itemize each and every expenditure, ranging from your own salary or draw to the postage and bank fees. Let me provide a list of the more typical expenses but the following is by no means all-inclusive:

- Accounting Fees
- Advertising
- Bad Debts
- Bank Charges (interest / fees)
- Business Travel
- Club Memberships
- Courier Fees
- Donations
- Insurance
- Inventory
- Janitorial

- Legal Fees
- Licenses
- Loan / Lease Payments
- Office Rent
- Office Supplies — general
- Phone / Fax (rentals, line charges, long distance, hook-up)
- Postage
- Printing
- Professional Association Fees
- Salaries — others (office, adjuncts, associates)
- Salaries — owner(s)
- Seminar / Convention Registration Fees
- Taxes
- Taxis
- Typing Services
- Vehicle

Company Cash Flow Projections

The cash flow projection is a means to show when income is received and when expenses are paid. In essence, you are taking the annual data from the projected income and expense statement and spreading the information over a period of time.

It is one thing to bill a client for work done. It is quite another matter when that invoice gets paid. If you have limited experience or knowledge of the paying habits of your potential clients, it is best to estimate payment in sixty to ninety days.

Your banker will be interested in the quality of your receivables. Put another way, are your targeted clients Fortune 500 types? Or are you likely to be dealing with relative unknowns where their ability to pay could be in question. This leads you into comments and observations concerning historical trends regarding potential bad debts or write-offs (see expense item in the projected income and expense statement).

In preparing the comments, you want input from your accountant. Your explanatory notes should outline all the assumptions you made when putting together the cash flow projection.

Request for Loan Accommodation

If your business plan is being prepared specifically to justify loan accommodations, the following pertinent items must be covered.

Term Loans

Term loans are generally granted for capital expenditures related to the purchase of equipment, furnishings and leasehold improvements. It is important to itemize the expenditures and layout the total cost. Then record the amount of assistance required and the preferred terms of repayment.

Be prepared to address the issue of how much equity your company (or you) will be putting up, and what you can offer as security or collateral. Discuss this topic with your accountant. (By the way, what your accountant thinks might be appropriate for security may not align with what your banker has to say.)

In the final analysis, banks will rely on you to repay them, even if the loan is in your company name. Be prepared to pledge some form of security that will be tied to your personal assets.

Operating Loans

Operating loans normally apply to financing receivables and/or work in progress. In preparing your business plan to substantiate this type of loan accommodation, you will be tying the amount requested to your cash flow projection.

Traditionally, operating loans are secured by an assignment of the actual receivables. Lenders apply certain ratios or margins to determine how much they will lend you against your receivables. The ratio will depend upon a number of factors, including the quality of receivables and the length of time the receivables are outstanding. For example, a bank might lend you 50 cents for every dollar of receivables (only receivables outstanding for 90 days or less will apply) to a maximum of a certain amount.

I used the expression "traditionally" in the last paragraph. You could discover your banker may request additional backup security for an operating loan associated with your newly formed company. Your business plan should clearly outline what security you are prepared to offer. Of course, your suggested security might well be open to debate by your banker.

In many situations, lenders and investors may want the business owner to arrange for and assign life insurance to provide blanket coverage for loans. This is not an uncommon request but you should review matters with your family, your accountant and insurance agent before including this type of security in any business plan.

Everyone should complete a business plan but the amount of work and the degree of detail will depend upon a number of factors. For some of us, going through the exercise is confirmation of what we already know we are going to do. Others will require the plan to arrange for crucially needed financing.

The benefits of compiling a business plan will accrue directly to you, the independent owner and operator.

CHAPTER 17

Focus, Organization, Research & Activity
Enjoy Your Adventures in Your New Venture

On a personal note, I hope you have found the preceding sixteen chapters informative and thought-provoking.

While writing the book, I reflected on my own mistakes. With luck and planning, you should avoid some of those pitfalls. I also tried to convey the approaches and ideas that have proven successful for myself and many of my consulting colleagues.

For the entrepreneur, there are no guarantees for success. Every consultant will have his or her own thoughts on what factors have contributed favourably to a positive result. But few will dispute that focus, organization, research and activity are key ingredients if you want to achieve the goals you have set for yourself, your family and your company.

Let me close with a favourite quote from Elbert Hubbard:

"Get your happiness out of your work, or you will never know what happiness is."

Good luck — your new venture is sure to be an adventure!

Reg Pirie

Mail / Fax Order Form

To: **Ink Ink Publishing**
       120 Promenade Circle - Suite 1107
       Thornhill, Ontario Canada L4J 7W9
       Tel: 416-230-3241
       Fax: 905-771-6668

Please send me one copy of From Starting to Marketing... YOUR OWN CONSULTING BUSINESS for $20.00. The price includes all taxes, handling and shipping. The book may be mailed to:

Name:_____

Address:_____

_____

City:_____

Province / State:_____

Postal / Zip Code:_____

Contact Ink Ink Publishing regarding larger orders. We would be pleased to provide a discount for volume purchases.

Payment Options:

1. **My $20 cheque, payable to Ink Ink Publishing, is enclosed.**

2. **Bill My Visa Account #:**_____

    Visa Expiry Date:_____

    Signature For Visa Purchases:_____

For lecture, seminar and guest speaking information, Reg Pirie may be reached by fax or phone at Ink Ink Publishing. Or email Reg Pirie directly at pirie@inforamp.net.